THE CREATORS FLEX, EMILE YX?

The Breakdancer Thinks & Takes Action

Emile Jansen

Heal The Hood Project Publishers

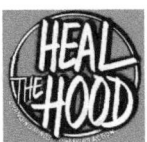

I dedicate this book to my family, friends and community. In the African tradition of elders pasisng information forward to future generations, I know that I am me because of everyone else. Everything that I have achieved is because of ALL who have contributed to my being. In the spirit of Ubuntu I thus THANK YOU ALL. To my children I show that we can do whatever we set our hearts and callings to.

INTRODUCTION

In the African tradition of introducing myself, I have to say that I am a result of all who have gone before me and all that I have done, is thus also as a result of the community and memory that makes me who I am. I am because of all who was, is and will be.

I decided to share this book that contains my actions or deeds, that were born from my thoughts and that are influenced by all that is around me. As a dancer, I pride myself in showing my minds creations before speaking about it. I have thought and then danced after hours of rehearsal and preparation. I do not enter the world without preparing myself and thinking and rethinking before doing.

This book highlights the many actions that I have taken over the years and it celebrates my successes, but more importantly exposes the many trials and errors that birthed these results. I introduce you to my deeds and know that they are higlights from 56 years of being on this planet in this form and 41 years of being introduced and falling in love with Hip Hop Culture and my creative self. I can honestly say that Hip Hop saved my life and showed me who I truly am and can be. It reawoke my Godself and demanded that I step into the circle as myself and know that it is a journey of discovery that travels through time and space.

Lastly, I have to tell you that the dancer is truly the physical manifestation of the word. We think and do.

My performance name is Emile YX? but I was born Emile Lester

Jansen on the 20th July 1968 in Peninsula Hospital, District 6, Cape Town, South Africa. I am the son of a primary school teacher, Emelda Lorna Jansen and an iconic soccer playing Dad, Basil *Puzzy* Jansen. I am thus a proponent of experiential education and also a qualified school**teacher**.

I write about my experiences as a naughty kid from Grassy Park in my book series, *A Colourful Life*. I have become very outspoken about the illusions of one story being told about my community and I demand that I keep myself accountable, by telling stories that reflect the realities of growing up during Apartheid in all its honesty and contradictions. Through it all we played sport, went to the movies, fell in love, got married and had children that would also go through it all. Growing up & experiencing the violence of the South African Apartheid state while still at school, is captured in this song & video. I have also written about it in *Captive Sunbeams* in my book *My Hip Hop is African & Proud.*

I am considered an elder of the South African Hip Hop community because I started breakdancing in 1982 with my group called *Pop Glide Crew.* We later went on to create the legendary South African Hip Hop Group named, **Black Noise** in 1988. Over the years I have played a major role in directing the groups *down time* to growing Hip Hop Culture throughout the Western Cape and later throughout South Africa. I have tried and try many new things, but I am best known for my activism, youth development work and community outreach projects. I later decided to separate these activities from the Black Noise performance group and started **Heal the Hood Project** in 1998.

Before that I attended the Universal Zulu Nation Anniversary in New York in 1994, where I met some of the founders of Hip Hop Culture like Afrika Bambaata, KoolDJ Herc, the Cold Crush Crew and many more. I was immediately impressed by the Do For Self mentality and honesty of many of these artists signed to huge labels.

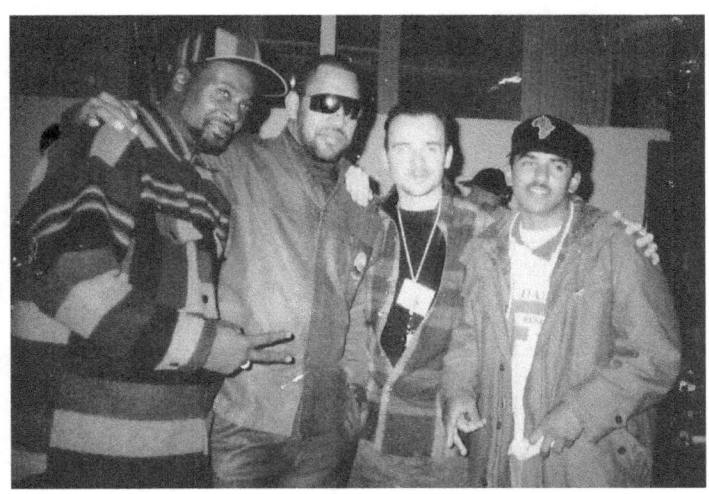

It was this experience that helped me to create numerous events like the first Universal Zulu Nation Anniversary in Kraaifontein in 1995, which became the African Battle Cry in 1996. The more I spread the breakdancing video that was sent to Cape Town by Storm & Swift from Battle Squad, who were also at the Zulu Nation Anniversary in New York, the more the culture started spreading outside of Mitchells Plain and the Cape Flats.

I would travel around to libraries to share the elements of Hip Hop Culture with anyone and everyone that would listen. This grew into library tours, Da Juice Hip Hop Magazine, African Hip Hop Indaba, Battle of the Year South Africa and many more events to keep youth positively active.

Our actions actually contributed to the growth of the entire Hip Hop Culture throughout Southern Africa. Eventualy this sharing would teach me how to teach outside of the schoolteacher background that I had. I started writing about Hip Hop to create our own newsletter, that became our first magazine and which spread our story globally as I exchanged magazines with underground Hip Hop heads throughout the world. All the while I was writing rhymes and performing with Black Noise Hip Hop Group. I blended the community service with the mission of growing the Hip Hop Culture throughout the country and created awareness of South African Hip hop in the global Hip Hop Community. I did this by writing to penpals and magazines throughout the world. This was before the internet.

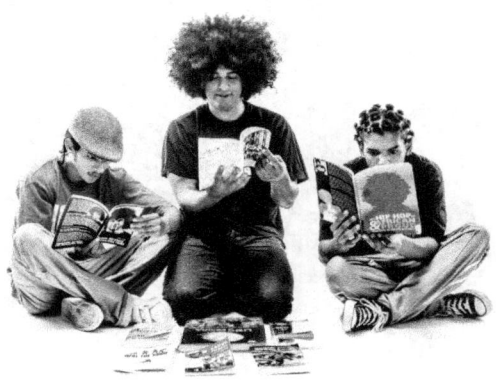

As I kept teaching in new places throughout South Africa, I saw that the skills are worthless when they amplify the self hate that we were and are being taught by colonial and capitalist powers. I created a practical Hip Hop school that served as a learning space for the expansion of the ideas into a sylabus that would then be taught by the very learners that I taught in schools throughout the Western Cape. I tested the content by having the members of **Mixed Mense** and others who learned from me, teach it globally. The syllabus I created is currently being taught in 14 schools (1500 learners weekly) encouraging alternative information about Africa that develops **Self-Worth, Self-Love & Pride**. The course culminates in learners creating songs containing art, dance & music videos. I have been spending the last five years documenting the lessons I have learned and sharing my findings in books, plays, songs, documentaries, childrens books and other learning materials. Creating this booklet from my biography is an important introduction via this platform.

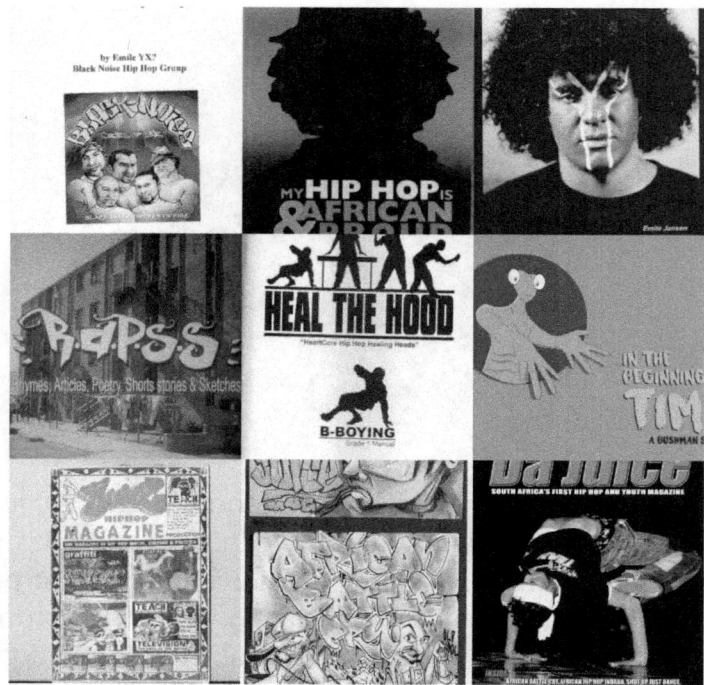

THE DANCER

I started b-boying (Breakdancing) for *Pop Glide Crew* in 1982 & I am thus seen as a pioneer of South African Hip Hop. In 1984 *Pop Glide Crew* won their first competition at Route 66, Town Centre, Mitchells Plain.

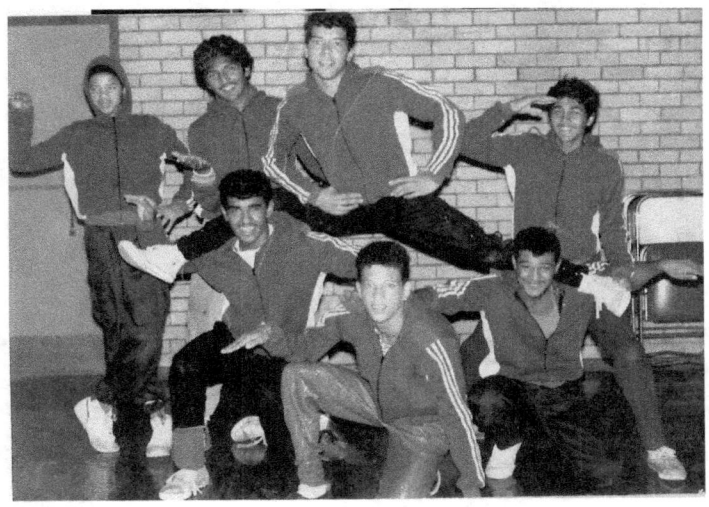

In 1994 I started spreading B-boying throughout South Africa by teaching and creating events. As I spread the dance throughout the Western Cape and then nationally, I encouraged young dancers to travel to each others neighbourhoods and often even transported them from one community to another to host battles. The culture crew very quickly with the sharing of VHS tapes to various communities and as soon as we hosted African Battle Cry, which culmunated in a focused competition in the various elements of the culture, it established the entire culture in the consciousness of Cape Town Hip Hoppers understanding of Hip Hop Culture. I found out about Battle Of The Year and took a chance to apply to Winnie Mandela, who was the Minister of Arts & Culture, Science and Technology, for funding and she responded positively.

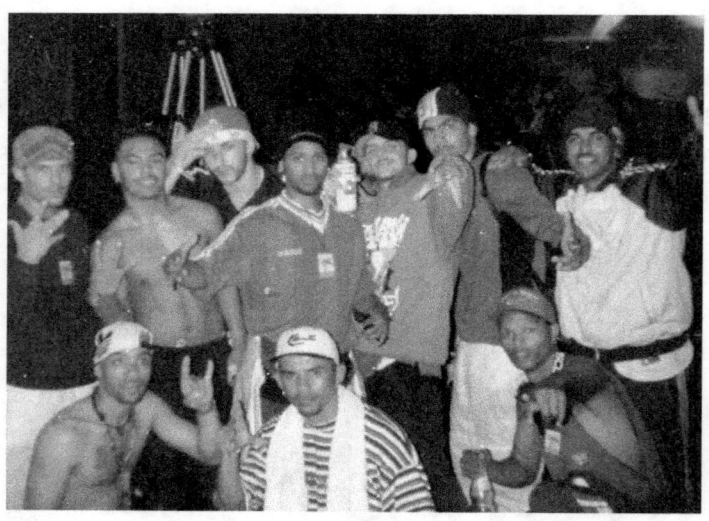

We travelled to Germany, to mostly perform at the event and then entered without much hope of making it to the final battles. Black Noise Crew won 3rd place at the World Champs at *Battle Of The Year* in Germany in 1997. We returned to teach others and give others the same opportunity. In 2000 I managed the South African All-star team that won 4th place at Battle Of The Year in 2000.

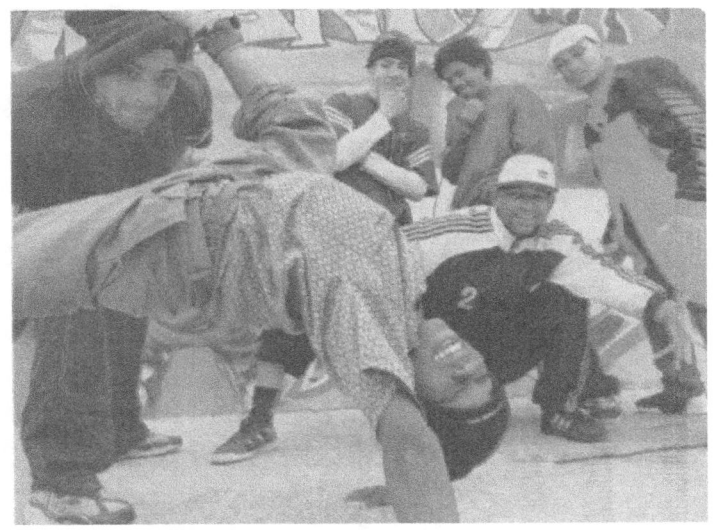

From 1997 – 2008 I helped Heal The Hood Project fund-raise to send more than 250 of our best Hip Hop artists to international events like touring to Namibia, Botswana, Zimbabwe, Heal The Hood Project Sweden, Denmark, Finland, Heal The Hood Project Norway, England and Italy with the *Womad Festival*, *Battle Of The Year* in Germany, *R16* in Korea, *Red Bull BC One* in Brazil & India, *Trinity International Hip Hop Festival* in the USA and *IBE* in The Netherlands.

From 2011 – 2013 I judged a reality dance show on ETV called *Step up Or Step Out.* In 2020 I decided to be open to learning other peoples techniques of teaching Breaking and I graduated from the *B-boy & B-Girl Dojo's First International Teacher Education Certificate.*

EMILE JANSEN

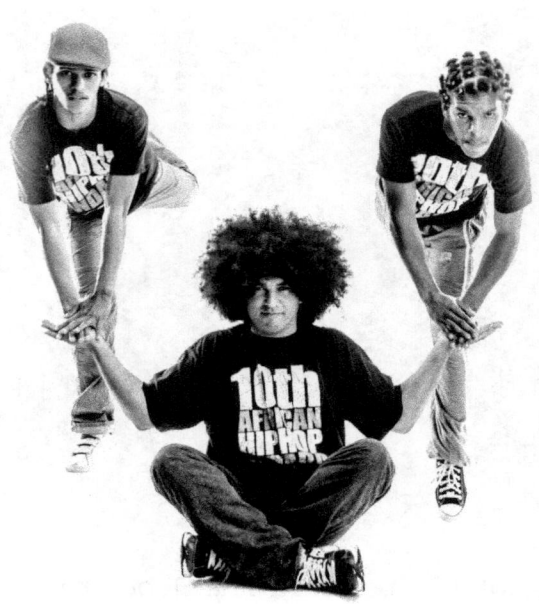

THE MC / RAPPER

In 1988 I co-founded *Black Noise Hip Hop Group* which consisted of the remainder of the 1980's B-boys from various breakdance crews like Pop Glide Crew, Supreme Team Crew, Jam Rock Crew, Ballastic Rock Crew and Cape Town City Breakers. It was when one of our founder members and rapper left the group that we decided to firstly maintain the element of dance in the crew and later created an all elements Hip Hop crew.

It was while I was writing about my 42 years of falling in love with Hip Hop Culture and recalling amazing stories for my 4 part book series called *Making A Black Noise*, that the idea of releasing related books came to life. In fact, I have since decided to release a book containing each albums lyrics, ideas and situations that birthed the songs as well as pictures that show the recording and touring related to the albums. As an MC or Rapper, I wish to show others that what we create can take many forms and not only empower us, but also the many who read the realities of being an artist and how to diversify our creative income streams by creating various platforms on which our creations can live and be revived for future generations to enjoy and learn from. To quote a friend of mine, "Rhymes, Songs and Beats do not get rotten. They can always be renewed and repurposed for future egenrations and once again feed you."

As Black Noise Hip Hop Group we recorded and released **13 Black Noise albums** including ***Pumpin' Loose Da Juice*** (1992), which was released by Tusk records, which was a subsidary of Gallo Records. Our first signing to a record label was a huge eye opener.

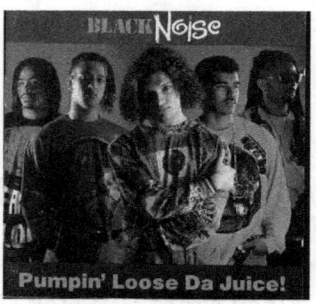

We then independently released **Rebirth Of Mind & Hip Hop Culture** (1993), *Black Facts* (1994), *Rebirth CD* (1995),

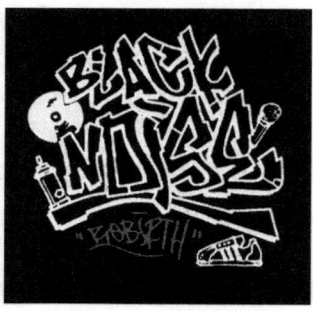

Questions (1996), *Hip Hop Won't Stop* (1998), **Circles Of Fire (2000),**

Rotational High (2002),

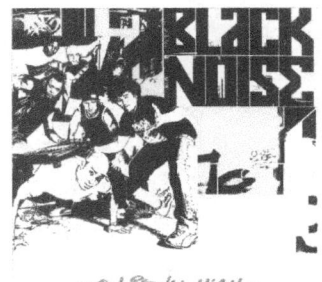

Jam Sessions (2004), *Getcha On The Floor* (2006), *Best Of Black Noise* (2008), **Stone Garden Soldiers (2010)**

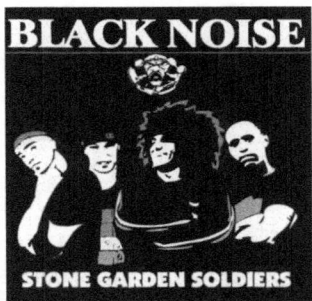

and **Black Noise Matters (2019)**.

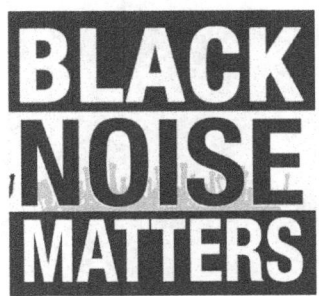

I also recorded & released **15 solo *Emile YX?* Albums**:-

Who Am I? **(2003)**,

***Conquering Lions* (2006),**

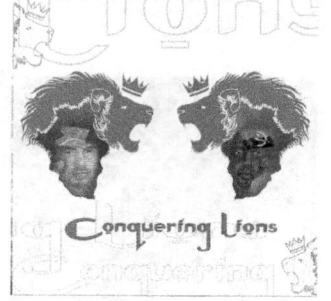

***Roar – Live it Loud* (2008),**

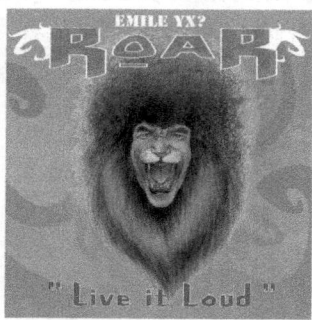

***Conscious Rhymes For Unconscious Times* (2010),**

Afrikaaps soundtrack (2011), *Born & Bred of the Cape Flats* (2012), *Mixed Mense* (2013), **Take Our Power Back (2015),**

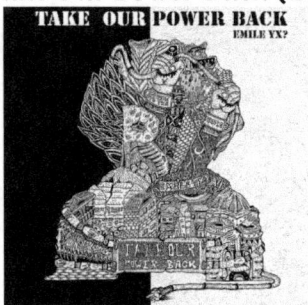

Demockery (2016),

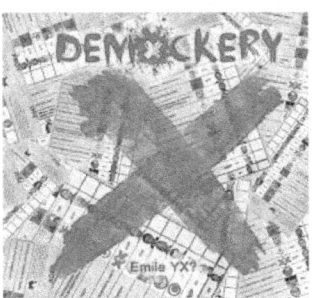

From B-boys To Being Men (2016),

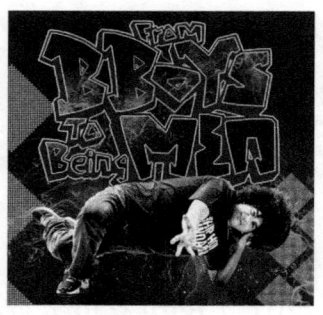

***Songs & Stories For My Son* (2017),**

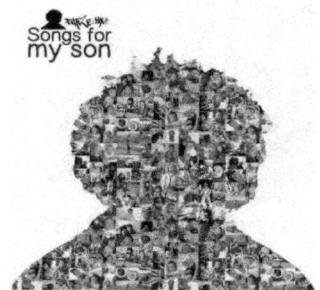

***Songs & Stories for my Daughter* (2018),**

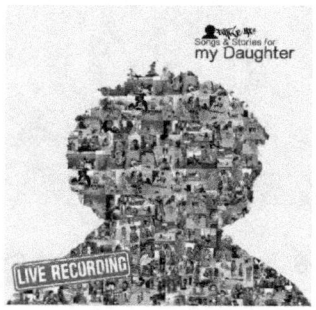

***Afrocentric* (2018),**

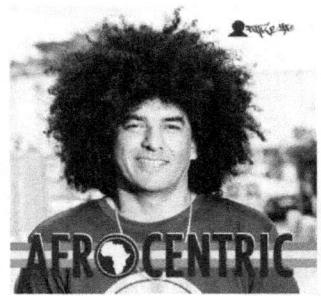

Kaapse Katte (2019)

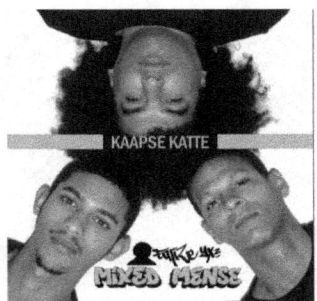

& *Billion Hair* (2022).

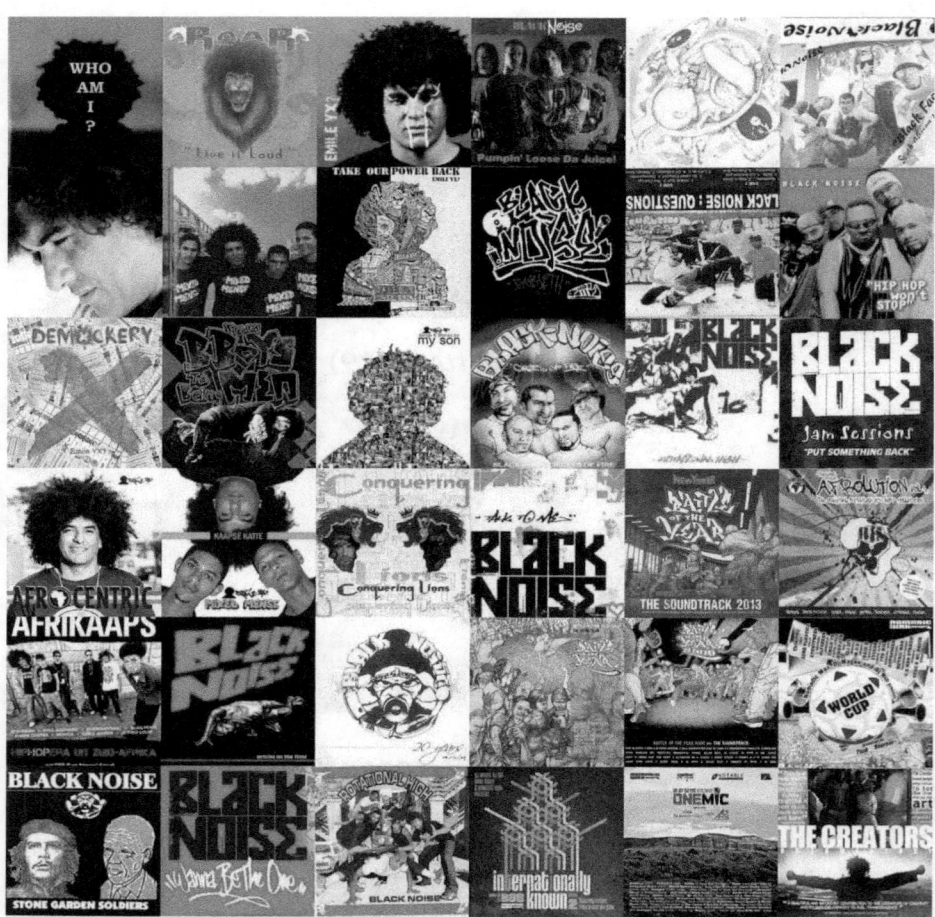

If that were not enough, I featured on **13 compilation albums** like *Monster Hits* (1992),

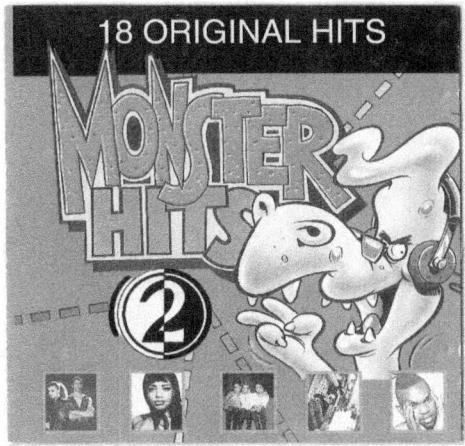

***Do For Self* Compilation (1994)**,

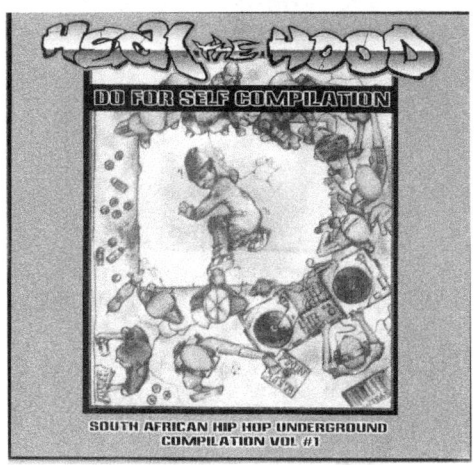

A Moment In Cape Town (2001),
***Battle Of The Year* Compilations (2000, 2001 & 2013)**,

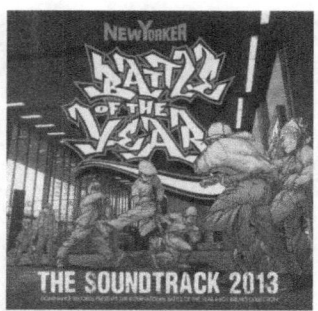

Afro-lution Compilation (2004), *Baobab Tree* Compilation (2005), *Mother City* Compilation (2007),

***Anti-World Cup* (2010)**,

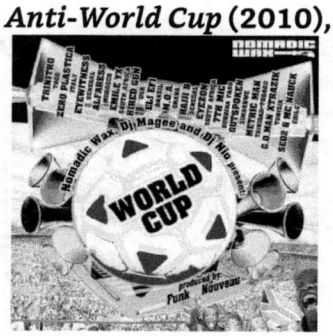

***Internationally Known 2* (2012)**,

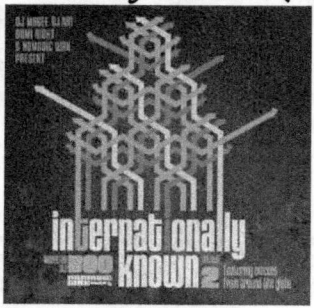

***Fees Must Fall* (2015)** and *Pangea: Hip Hop Heals* (2021).

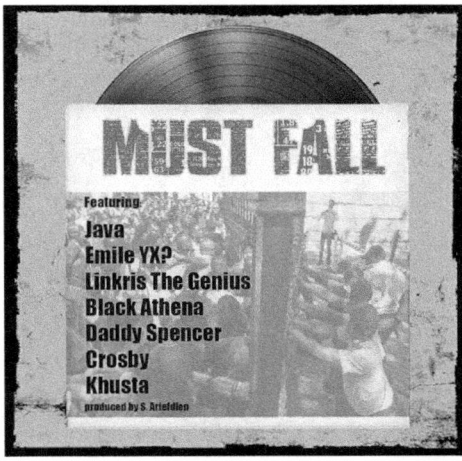

Since the very start of our Do For Self mentality, I have helped Heal The Hood Project to release **7 Heal the Hood compilation albums**

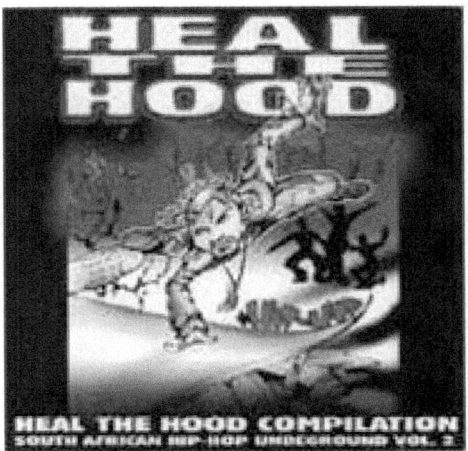

and also assisted **6 local artists release** their solo albums. Artists like *Plain Madnizz,* **Isaac Mutant,**

EMILE JANSEN

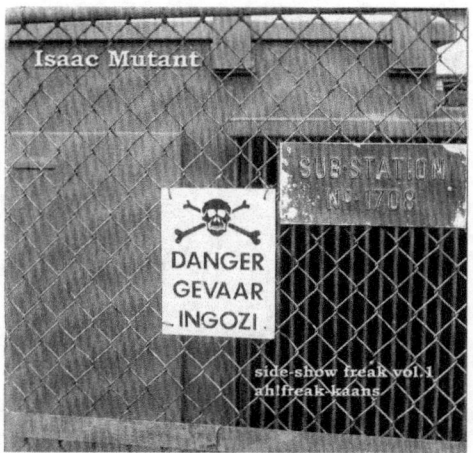

Lionz of Zion, **Ancient Men,** Jamayka Poston, Resistencia

THE AUTHOR

In 1990, with the help of other members of Black Noise and Desiree Van Den Heever, I created Black Noise News (BNN), which was the foundation for creating South Africa's first Hip Hop Magazine *Da Juice* in 1993. It was originally called *The Message* because of the song by the same name by *Grandmaster Flash and The Furious Five* that spoke about Africa and made me realise that I could tell my own stories.

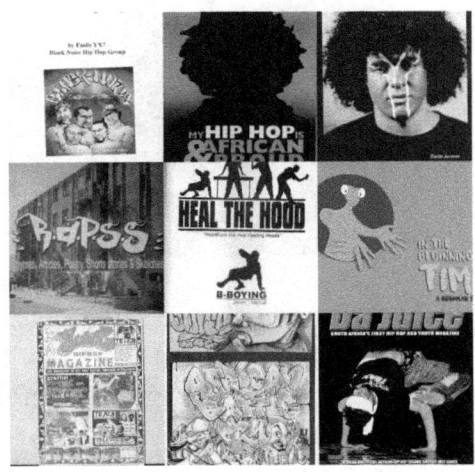

I have since written and contributed to 28 books:

(1) **What is Hip Hop?**, I wrote in response to youth asking that very question when we toured libraries throughout the Western Cape. I gave a local history, names and basics for getting started in

each of the elements of Hip Hop Culture. It was a cut and paste / photocopies book that I released to interested libraries and youth. Libraries would call me for copies because kids were stealing sections from the book or even the entire book.

(2) *My Hip Hop is African & Proud*, I wrote this book while I was on tour in Sweden and Norway. It was an answer to the originality of South African Hip Hop Culture and the lessons that I learned from Hip Hop Culture over the years. It allowed me to search within myself to explain how Hip Hop helped me to find myself and then also share pride building information with others so that they can do the same.

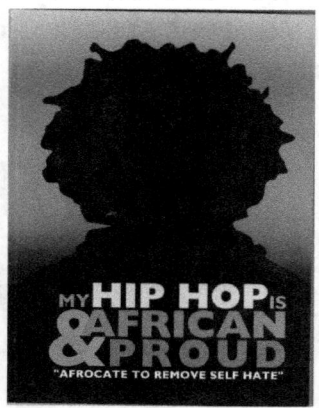

(3) **Conscious Rhymes For Unconscious Times**, was written after hearing a call from Hip Hop Elders in the USA to not complain about how one story of violence, drugs, commercialization and negativity is being told about Hip Hop Culture and people of colour and that the only way to change that was to write our own books, rap our own songs in the spaces that we have control over in order to balance this perspective and divisive attitude of corporate controlled media.

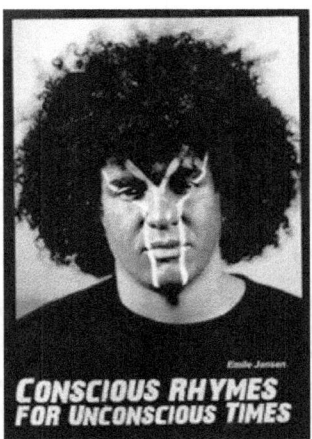

(4) **Heal The Hood B-boying Grade 1 Manual**, was created when I was teaching a new generation how to teach and after they qualified, I gave each learner a copy of the book in order to keep their lesson ideas frewsh and to ensure that the lessons that I share dwith them would not be lost. It served as an introduction or foundation to the basics of Breaking in order for them to build on in the future.

(5-7) **R.A.P.S.S. version 1-3** (Rhymes, Articles, Poetry, Short Stories and Sketches) After writing and releasing my own books, it was time to help others do the same. As the acronym says, we supplied a platform for people to share their stories and then helped others to print their own books by sharing the ease with which this is truly possible. We explained to rappers that they are writers and how they could print their creations. We asked people to write about our events and what the experience was like and that became the articles. We gave space for poets to share their work with our learners. We found hundreds of people who were writing short stories and even more sketching and doing aerosol art and supplied this platform for their work to be seen in our schools and visitors who bought the books and then we would plough the money into the next issue of the book.

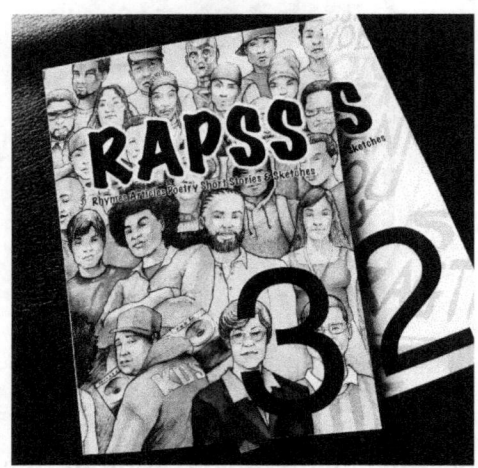

(8) *Land i Forandring* & (9) *Barn och unga i sodra Afrika* are books that Swedish authors and educators were releasing and while I was touring Sweden, they asked me to write about issues of land/country transformation and what I thought was needed in the education world in order for things to change in South Africa.

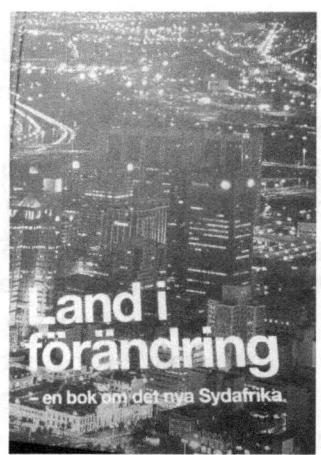

(10) *Munscen Wie Du & Ich, is a compilation of stories from people throughout the world who had experienced life changing moments in*

their lives. It is an amazing book with amazing pictures and stories of amazing people.

(11) I Praise Dance, was a research project on various dance styles in Cape Town and South Africa that I was asked to contribute to around the topic of Hip Hop dance in Cape Town and my relationship with the community.

(12) Their Stories With my Debut Album Tracy Chapman, was created to celebrate the 30th Anniversary of Tracy Chapmans Debut album, they asked her fans to write bout our experience with her album. My story was selected on the 5th April 2018.

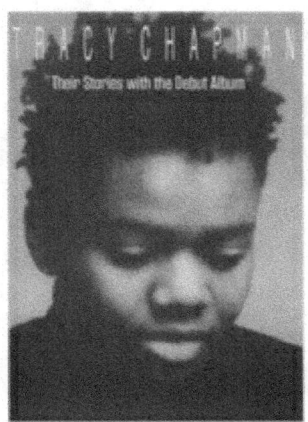

(13) Bushman Creation Story, I had read somewhere and then decided to illustrate the story as a childrens book for my son. Others saw it and I decided to create little booklets for others as well. Here are the names of other illustrated booklets and stories that I created for my son and daughter.

(14) *The Story Of The Wind*, (15) *Fire The Dancer*, (16) *Princess Vlei*, (17) *The Big Water-snake*, (18) *The Lioness*, (19) *Sally the Salmon*, (20) *Why Turtles Cry*, (21) *Saartjie Baartman*, (22) *Girl That Made The Milky Way*,

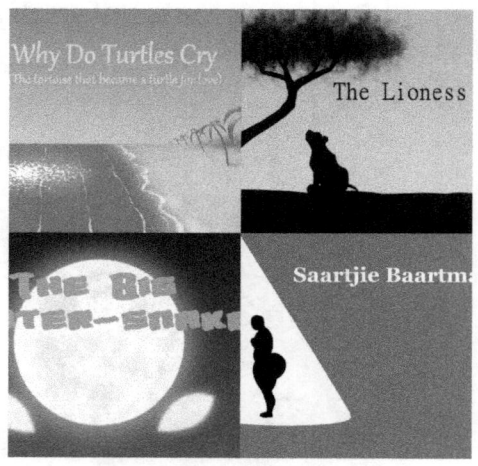

(23) *Reflections on Knowledge Learning & Social Movements*, Dr Paul Hendricks, a good friend of mine was approached by other academic friends working on this book about learning and social movements. Aziz Choudry (MHSRIP) and Salim Vally are reknowned academics and I was a bit hesitant to contribute, but Paul helped word the section I wrote appropriately for the audience it was aimed at.

(24) *The Hip Hop Cook Book*, was a result of my connection to the German event Battle Of the Year and my days of writing to Hip Hop Family throughout the world. Gerry Cutmaster GB Bachmann asked me to supply a South African recipe that he could create and add to this book of global Hip Hop pioneers favourite recipes. Released 15th September 2012.

(25) *Reconnect the String* was released in 2021 after being edited by Dr H.Samy Alim, Dr Donielle Prince and Dr Casey Wong. This book dissects the African Origins of Hip Hop Culture and its Ancestral Healing power. I weave real life experiences into the research and lessons learned.

(26) *A Colouredful Life.* "A Colouredful Life: Part 1 - The Naughty Kid Years (Die Stoutgat Jare)" offers a unique perspective on the experience of being labeled 'Coloured' during the Apartheid era in South Africa. In this collection of short stories, we delve into my early life and is set against the backdrop of Grassy Park, Cape Town. Within these pages, I share 24 carefully selected stories that encompass the very fabric of my upbringing. We journey from my birth to my parents, family, and the tight-knit community that shaped my formative years. The stories touch on key aspects of my early life, from the neighborhood I was born into (Waar ko' djy vandaan) to the profound importance of greeting in my community (groet is 'n moet). The tales explore themes of resourcefulness, sharing, and even the audacious act of pilfering food (kos gangsters). It is a heartwarming and hilarious journey into a world that may be foreign to some but is filled with universal themes of laughter, growth, and the shared experiences of childhood.

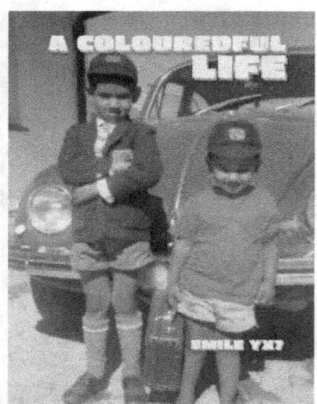

(27) *Neva Again* with UCLA Professor H. Samy Alim & South African Professors Adam Haupt from UCT & Quentin Williams from UWC. I contributed a chapter and assisted with the editing and artist participation.

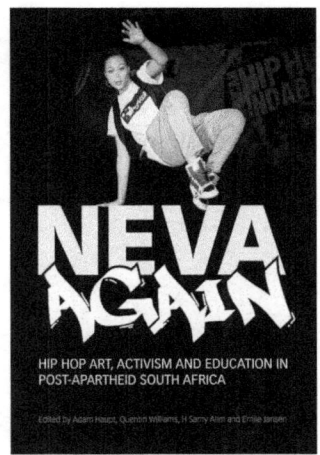

(28) *Freedom Moves*, edited by H. Samy Alim, Jeff Chang, and Casey Wong on the University of California Press (2022). I edited a lecture on the 5th Element of Hip Hop that Shaheen Ariefdien and I did at Stanford.

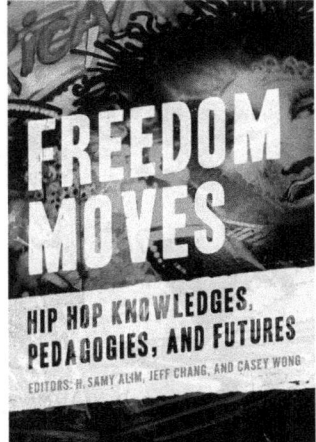

(29) Applied Linguistics, Volume 44, Issue 3, May 2023, Pages 576–584, Public Applied Linguistics in Action: A Conversation Between Emile YX? Jansen and Quentin Williams on Hip Hop Culture & Activism, Afrikaaps, Indigeneity, and Decolonial Futures

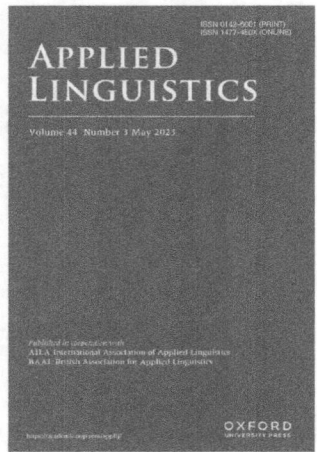

(30) Global Hip Hop Studies. I wrote an article on the *Breaking the normalization of appropriation and exploitation*.

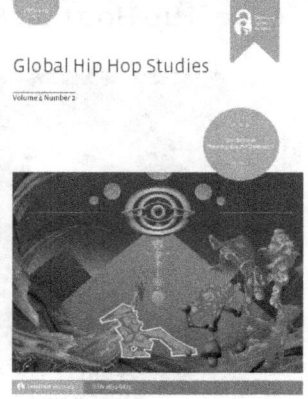

I am currently working on books named *Creating Solutions Part 1*, **Afrocation**, *Making A Black Noise, Heal The Hood: What Hip Hop Taught & Teaches Us, Hip Hop Cultural Education: We Live This, The Trilingual Dictionary of Afrikaaps* and *A Colouredful Life Part 2*.

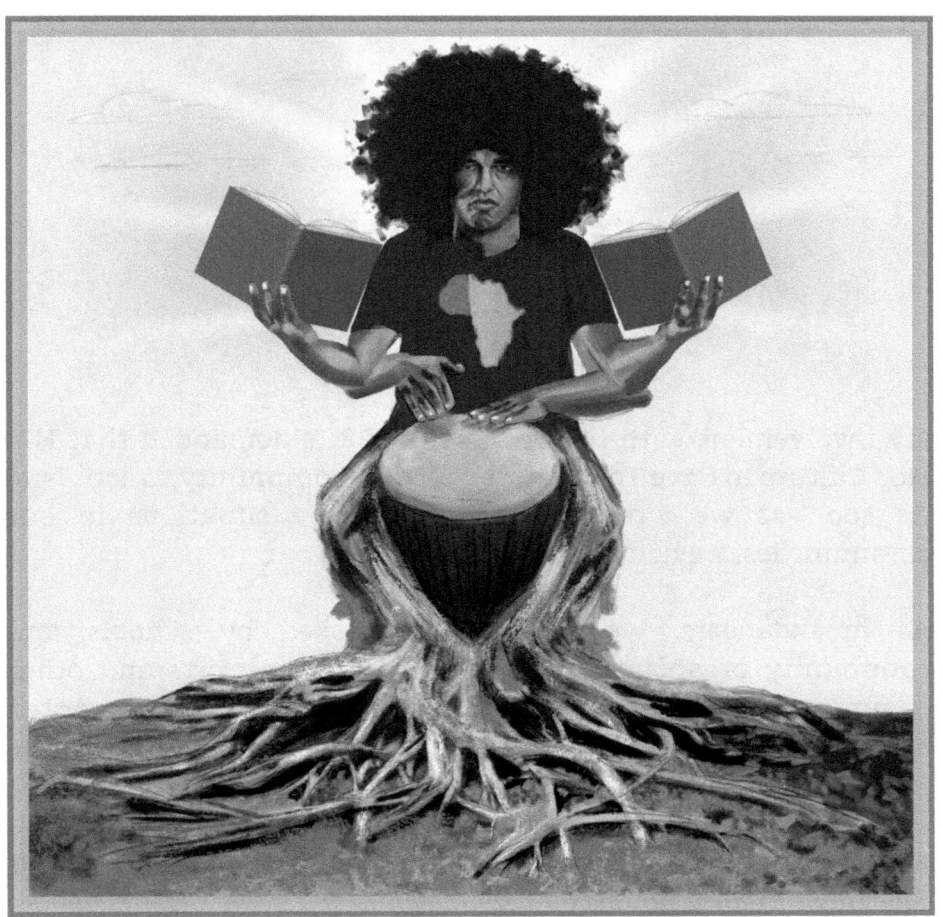

Afrocation

COMMUNITY ACTIVISM

My involvement with politics in the 1980's demanded that Hip Hop Culture in Cape Town motivated our community to activism. As soon as we wrote rhymes about the situations in our communities, we had to take action.

As breakdancers, we were always asked by schools and community organizations to "help out" at concerts and other community events to raise funds. This is a **deeply rooted community support system** that is often over-looked by the current mental poverty that is marketed and prevalent in these very same communities. I feel that **capitalism** has to **sell hopelessness** and only itself as the overnight way out of that **marketed mental poverty.**

In 1991, while I was teaching at Battswood Primary, I saw that Peninsula Feeding Scheme was having problems with funds to feed learners at various schools and I suggested that Black Noise participate in a series of fundraising concerts called, ***Rap To The Rescue.*** Later, we were asked by the local libraries to participate in their Holiday Programmes & tours to motivate and teach kids to read.

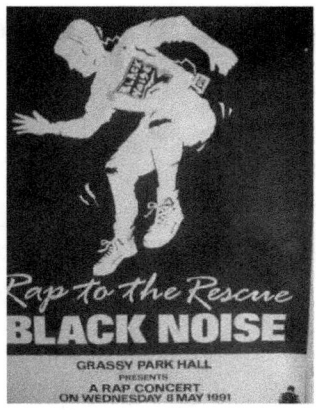

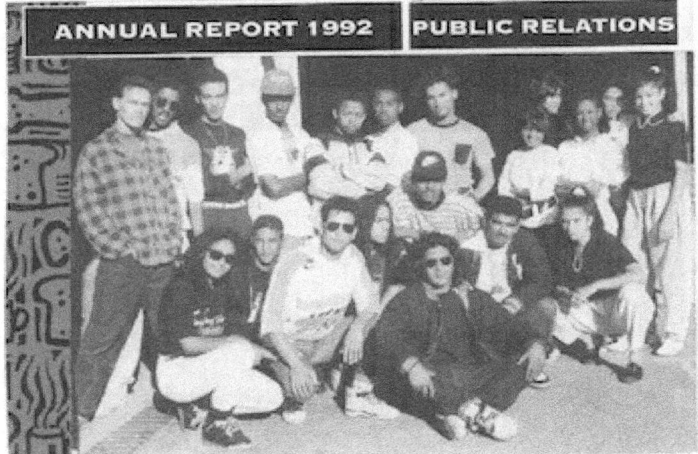

Peninsula Feeding Scheme Concerts

It was on this tour that I realised how little peope actually knew about Hip Hop Culture and the need for these libraries to have information about Hip Hop Culture, which birthed my book that answered the dominant question asked by kids at all the libraries we attended. "*What is Hip Hop*?" This was followed by another tour of teaching them the elements of Hip Hop Culture (*What is Hip Hop? Library tour*, which co-insided with my photocopied/ cut and paste style book. It was this tour that officially introduced the Western Cape to the culture and the ability to grow breakdancing into the Battle of The Year, South Africa and thus also bringing the awareness to the other dance forms associated to Hip Hop Culture.

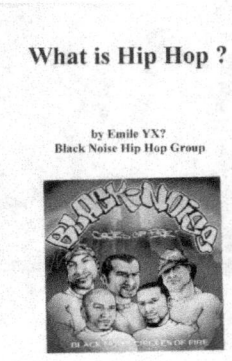

After I returned from **Universal Zulu Nation Anniversary** in New York and speaking to Afrika Bambaata & Black Consciousness group AUZAR, I realised that we had to create **Do For Self Concerts and Compilations.**

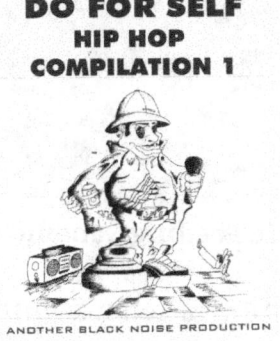

It was only in 1998 that I formalized the work that I was initiating into the NPO called *Heal the Hood Project.* Our activism and community outreach would be rewarded when Heal the Hood Project won the **Words, Beats & LIfe award** for the the *Best Hip Hop Organization* in in the world in 2010.

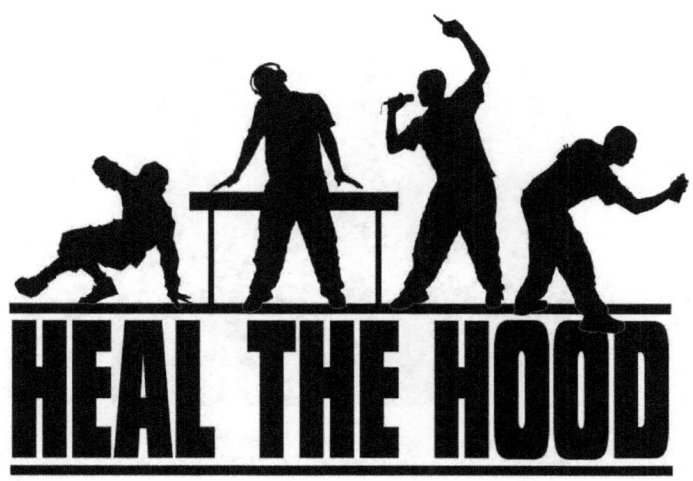

As a qualified schoolteacher, I brought education into South African Hip Hop and **helped raise funds for more than *250 artists* to travel to international events.** This was a reminder to others that if I could mobilize this collective economic power of our community, then so too can they. Aisde from my actions showing or teaching people what is possible, I went on to teach many others *how to teach* in order to spread the dance.

In 2005, I created a **Heal The Hood Practical Hip Hop School** with young dancers from Lavender Hill. This pilot project would create a perfect learning opportunity for the youth, but also for me to see how **Hip Hop Cultural Education** would benefit the community when implemented in the schools.

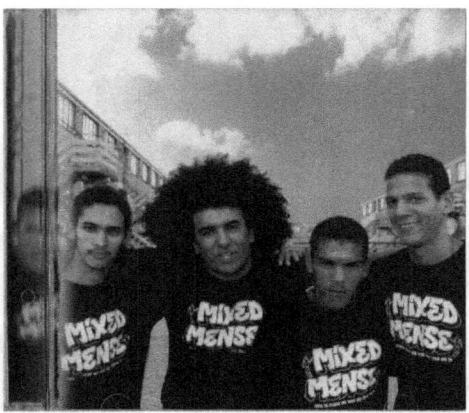

Heal The Hood Project is currently in 14 schools throughout the Western Cape and in 2025 we plan to expand the project to other provinces and Southern African.

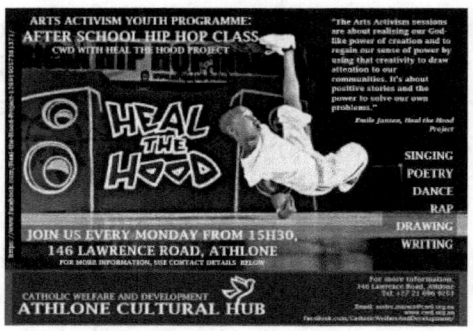

EVENTS

In 1991, as a member of Black Noise and a schoolteacher, I assisted Peninsula Feeding Scheme to raise funds to feed school children in Cape Town. I have also been a strong proponent of collective action and assisted the local Hip Hop community in hosting events like the *Power Jam* in Mitchells Plain. In 1993, as a member of Black Noise, we created:-

Do For Self Concerts to help schools raise funds, while supplying performance spaces for the local Hip Hop Community. Events were hosted in Grassy Park, Retreat and Mitchells Plain. Money was raised for Peninsula Feeding Scheme and for some schools that needed funds.

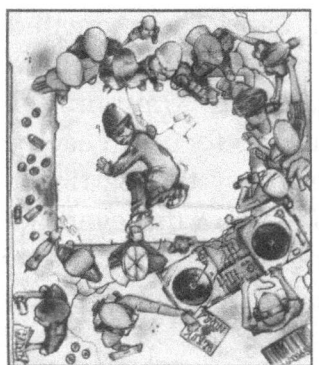

In 1995 I hosted the South African version of the *Universal Hip Hop (Zulu) Nation Anniversary*, which later became the *African Battle Cry,*. This event has become an annual event that serves as an end of year celebration of all the elements of the Hip Hop Culture in Cape Town, South Africa. It has even influenced Osmic

Menoe to create a similar event in Gauteng called Back To the City. African Battle Cry is usually hosted in December Holidays.

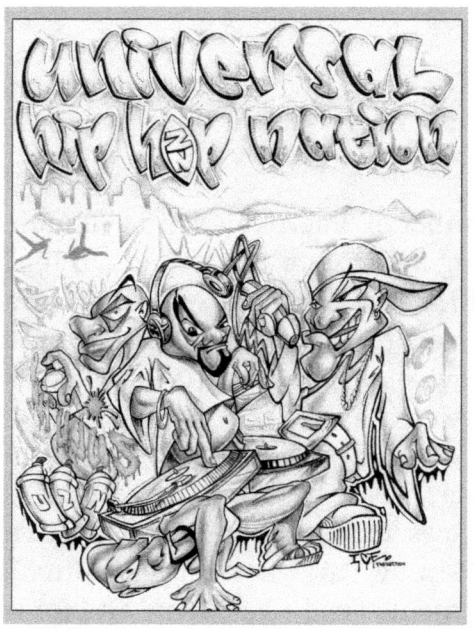

African Hip Hop Indaba,
In 2000, the City of Cape Town created a "Big Events" fund and encouraged the community to come up with events that showcased the best that our communities had to offer. I saw it as a perfect opportunity to focus on each of the elements of Hip Hop Culture and then host the Battle of the Year, as a fundraiser as part of the bigger 4/5 day event, which culminated in an award ceremony. Each year we host battles in each of the Hip Hop elements. We host this event around August/ September.

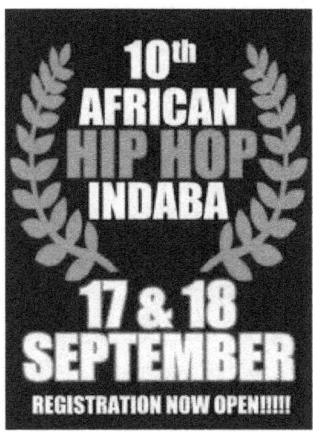

Battle of the Year South Africa,
After Black Noise won 3rd place in Germany in 1997, we first took one dancer along in 1998. It became our annual national competition to send a South African team.

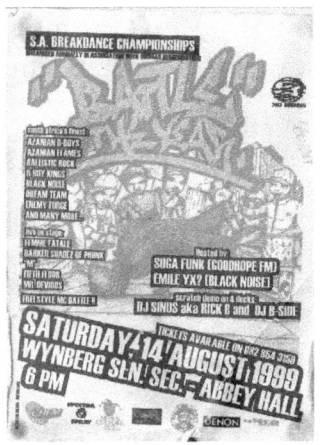

Shut Up Just Dance,
As the Hip Hop dancers increased in Cape Town, we saw it necessary to create more regular events for them to keep active. Shut Up Just Dance is hosted early in the year.

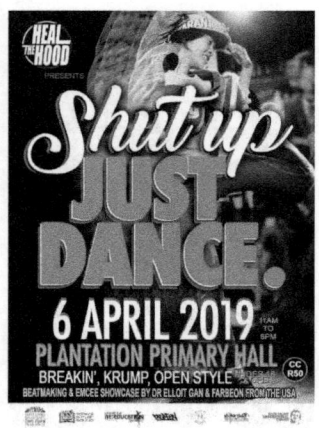

Cape Flats Uprising,
This event was initiated as a showcase of Cape Flats talent in the City of Cape Town. We negotiated a monthly date for the event and it served as a **fund-raiser for Heal The Hood Project to buy its own vehicle.** The selection of featured artists and DJ's also created job opportunities for the Hip Hop Community at the event, while often exposing the City of Cape Town to the talent they were very seldom exposed to.

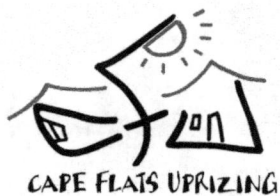

Learn To Surf Day,
This is a partnership with World Big Wave Surfing Champion, Cassiem Collier aka Cazz and Heal The Hood Project to give youth from the Cape Flats a unique and sometimes, once in a lifetime opportunity to learn to surf.

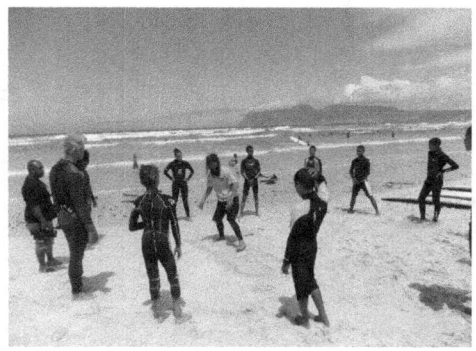

Up The Rock,
This event was first hosted when we realised that young people who lived in Cape Town, but never had the opportunity to climb the mountain. We partnered with some mountaineering clubs who gave youth the opportunity to sleep over on the mountain.

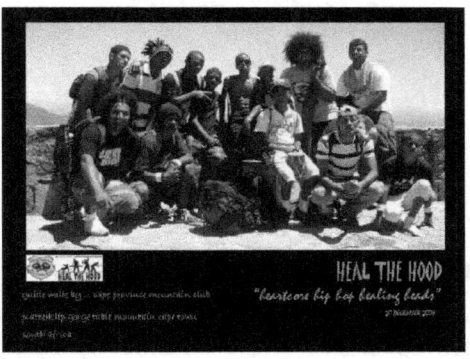

Cape Flats Film Festival,
After creating our own documentaries, *From B-boys To Being Men* and *Afrikaaps*, we started realizing that many people created documentaries, but never returned to our communities to show them to the very people that were featured in them. I partnered with another Afrikaaps cast member, Janine Blaq Pearl Van Rooy and we toured 30 schools showing our documentaries and also sharing locally created music videos.

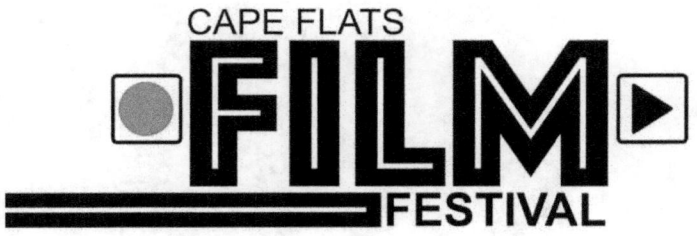

Positive Poster Week,
We countered the negative media that was being sold to youth from the Cape Flats by local media houses that told one story about our community. It was a very divisive remnant of the Apartheid regime to dehumanize people.

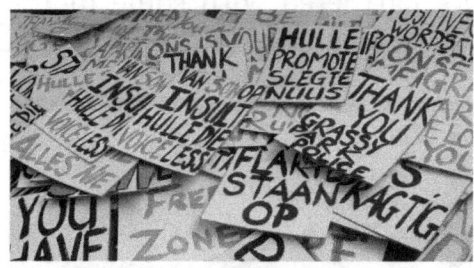

Cape Flats Performing Arts Conference,
In keeping with the Cape Flats Film Festival, we decided to gather some local artists to share their reality of beng artists in Cape Town and the national reality that they were faced with.

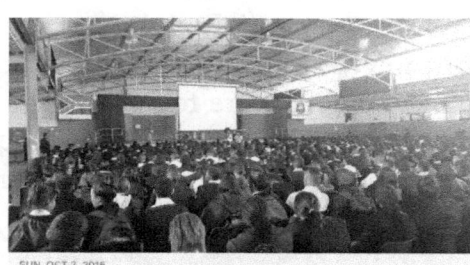

Cape Flats Cellphone Picture Competition

Is aimed at creating an alternative narrative about our community and demanding that we challenege the one story being told about us. These pictures are shared on our social media platforms.

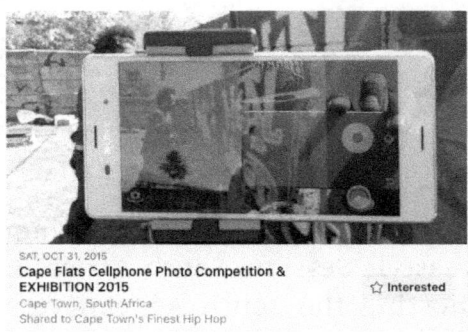

Our Hip Hop Festival,

We wanted to create a new showcase of the local Hip Hop community to the City of Cape Town at the town hall. We selected establised and up-and-coming local Hip Hop Cultural artists to showcase.

Reconnect the String,

After writing this book, I decided to interview elders of the Cape Town Hip Hop community and share their stories online. We were losing many elders during covid and these conversations really helped. I intend to keep doing this and sharing the interviews online and in book form.

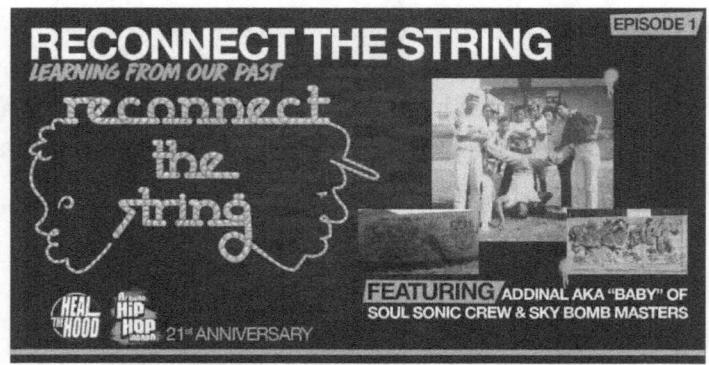

Freestyle Session South Africa and *R16*,
This event was born out of the eliminations and national finals we hosted for Freestyle Session, South Africa. After speaking to CrosOne about hosting the South African version of Fresstyle Session, we invited Hong 10 and Johnjay to judge at this event. Johnjay is connected to Red Bull and R16 and offered us the opportunity to select a South African crew to represent our country in R16 Final in Korea. Unfortunately the winning team from Port Elizabeth were unable to get their passports in time and we had to send the runners up.

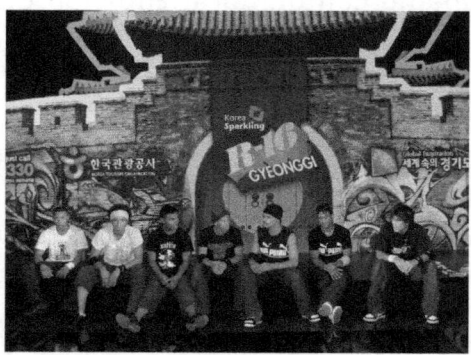

To Know Yourself is To Love Yourself National School Tour,
After hosting numberous Cape Flats Uprising events in the city and raising enough money to buy a vehicle, we decided to share Hip Hop Culture and knowledge of self nationally. We reached more than 150 000 learners throughout the country and shared

the lessons we learned nationally. These workshops exposed the national need for dialogue around issue of race, the illusions being sold by capitalism. We encouraged the power of self love as a solution to many of our countries problems. We also learned that race relations in South Africa was not being addressed and that Xenophobic attacks were imminant. We created an album called ***Human*** and discussions around the issue.

Human, Racism and Afrophobia Album & Workshops
One of the questions asked at all of the schools throughout "South Africa was "*All the Africans raise your hands?*", which showed South Africans deep sense of disrespect towards Africa that was taught and enforced by Apartheid, Colonialism and slavery to the population over many years.

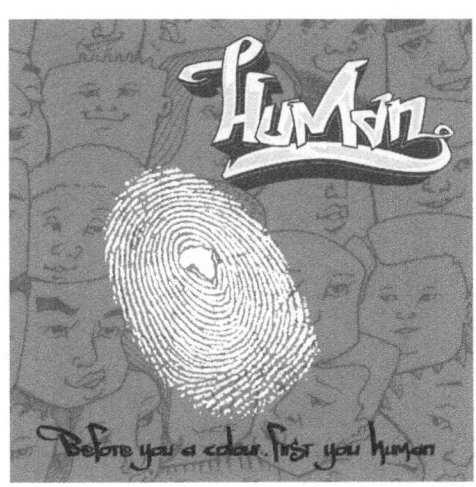

Black Noise Anniversary
We started hosting this event to celebrate the groups contributions to Hip Hop in South Africa and to ensure that young people learn that when they grow up, they can also look forward to being celebrated by the future generations. I have found that our society has a very short memory because colonialism and eurocentricity erased so much of our past heroes and sense of self.

EMILE JANSEN

In documenting our own stories and remembering, we empower ourselves and regain that sense of self that has been lost. Early in 2025 I will release part 1 of a 4 part book series that tells the stories of my lived experiences about my 42 years of "Making A Black Noise".

DOCUMENTARIES

I've been a participant in and created many documentaries:-

***Cape Of Hip Hop*,**
In the early 1990's Black Noise members in conjunction with Jeremy Hattingh and Nick Potgieter created this documentary as part of the creations of the Black Noise music videos of *His Story is Not For Me*, Life Ain't What It Used To Be and Hip Hop Won't Stop. It has interviews with King Jamo, Ray's Mom, Mr Fat, Shaheen & more.

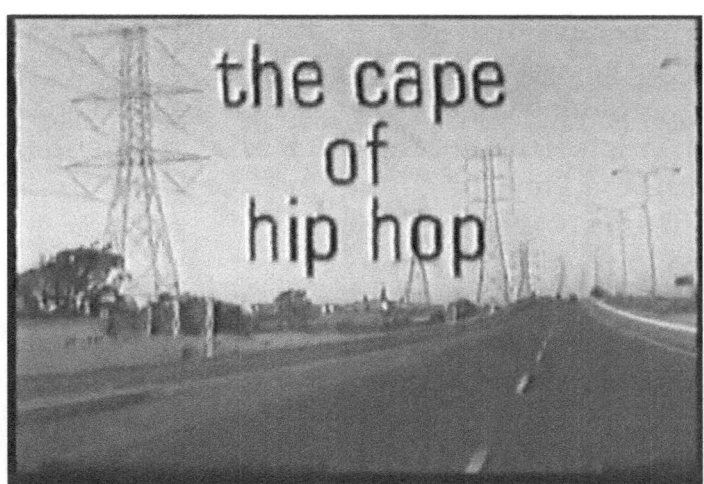

***Black Noise 20th Anniversary*,**
As part of our 20th Anniversary, I approached Beverly Mitchell to create a documentary that tells about the groups history to that point. Many of the members of Black Noise from different eras are questioned about their experience in the group. We have interviews with various members of Black Noise from each

collective over time to share their experience.

***Juvenis* - The GlobalGeneration celebrating UN 50th Anniversary,**
In 1995, Swedish documentary producer, Stefan Hilderbrand, toured South Africa and because Black Noise was signed to Making Music Management and Chris Syren (MHSRIP), we met with him and he added a scene of us in Mitchells Plain, that was later cut.

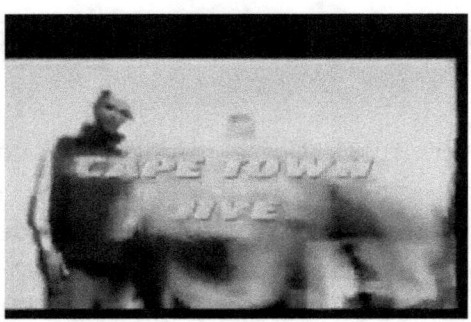

Cape Town Vibes,
This documentary had documentarians record Black Noise extensively and we did not see the story line, nor the final recording until long after it was released. To everyones surprize they had scripted the documentary as a comparison between Black Noise and Prophets Of Da City. I was not very impressed with the divisiveness of the producers.

The Creators,
Laura Gamse is a talented producer who showcased the work of various artists and my work with Heal The Hood Project was featured in the documentary. Many other South African artists were also featured and it can be seen on Tubi & Youtube Movies.

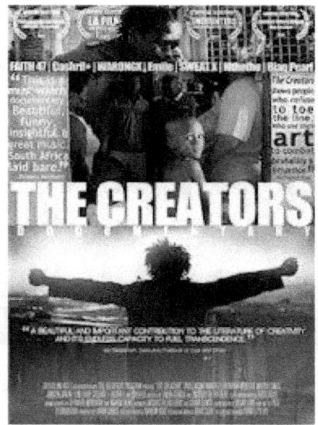

What Are We Doing Here?,
Two traveling film makers asked me to tag along during a day of doing workshops and shows in Cape Town. I remember them asking me questions and filming us and then they sent me the final documentation of their trip through Africa. It was an interesting take on what is truly happening on the continent and others perceptions of us.

From B-boys To Being Men,
My brother and I decided to re-edit a documentary that we wanted to create about the work that we do as Heal The Hood Project. We had asked someone else to edit the documentary, but soon realised that we would have to create it ourselves to truly capture the essence of what we had in mind.

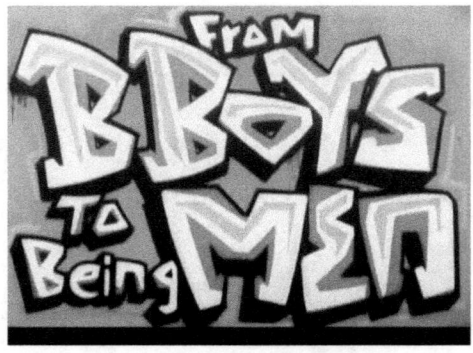

Bomb It (2 of my songs are featured in it),
Is a documentary about Aerosol Art around the world. I was approached by the documentarian to couple the South African Aerosol Art with my msuic. They selected two of my songs for the documentary.

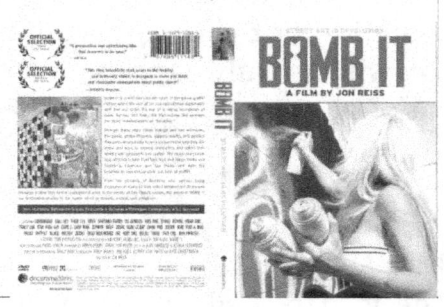

Afrikaaps,
In 2009 Catherine Henegan contacted me about her plans to create this story about the black history of Afrikaans. Initially I had no interest in being an actor, but as soon as I attended the briefing about the plays content and intention, I was completely engulfed in the potential that it had to enlighten young Cape Town children and repair their disconnect from their African heritage. We were given free range to create various songs to capture the content we wished to share. The play and the documentary of the play won numerous awards.

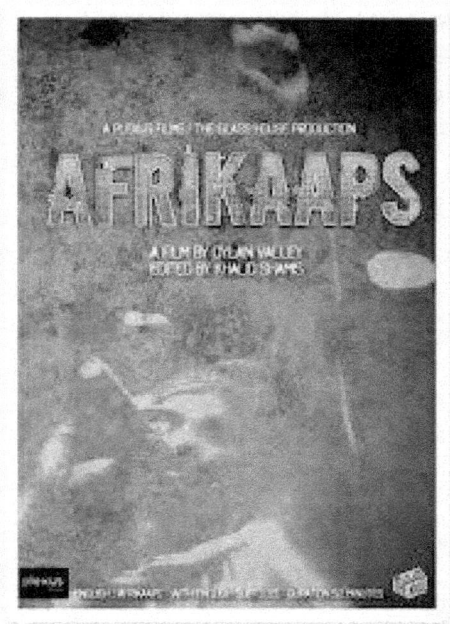

Emile YX? B-boy Basics,
In the mid 1990's I decided to record the basic B-boy moves that I taught at my workshops for others unable to attend.

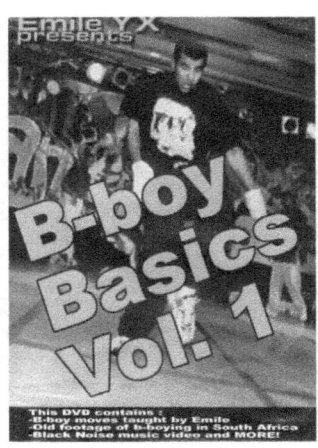

EMILE JANSEN

Coline & Robbie (wrote C.A.R.A Song for it),
C.A.R.A. (Coline Williams, Ashley Kriel, Robert Waterwitch and Anton Fransch) I wrote a song to honour them.

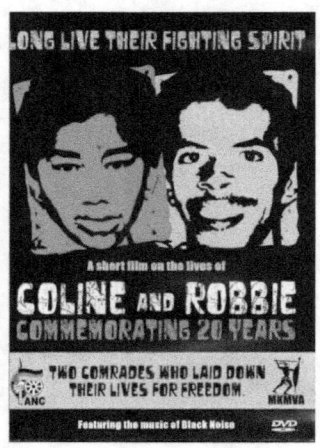

Dressing The Princess,
This documentary took place while we were fighting the City, Province and national politicians who allowed developers to build a mall on the banks of our beloved Princess Vlei. Princess Vlei Forum was created to protect the wetland & after protests the national and provincial political decision was reversed.

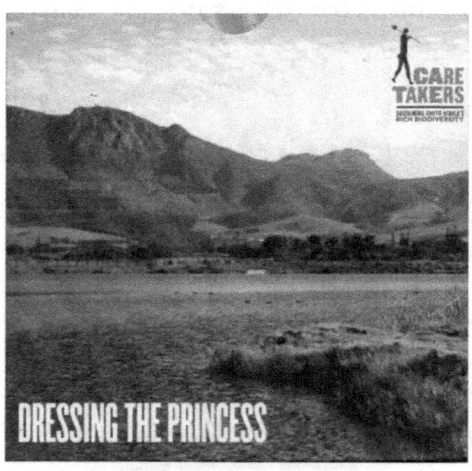

Break Like You,

THE CREATORS FLEX, EMILE YX?

Is about Breakings ability to encourage individuality and originality. It was the first time that I was approached to include my wife and son in the conversation.

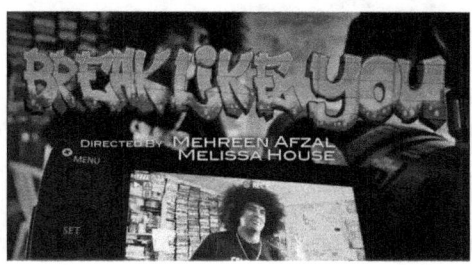

One Table Two Elephants,
This documentary is about my work with 2 young men from Lavender Hill & Heal The Hood Practical Hip Hop School called Mixed Mense. It is also set around the backdrop of our fight for Princess Vlei.

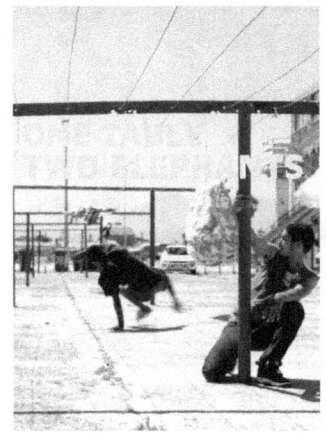

Tanne Trots (Returning our Teeth & Pride),
I attended a gorilla video production workshop at SAE Cape Town and as an outcome, we created a mini documentary called "Tanne Trots", about Bushman influence on so-called coloured people.

49

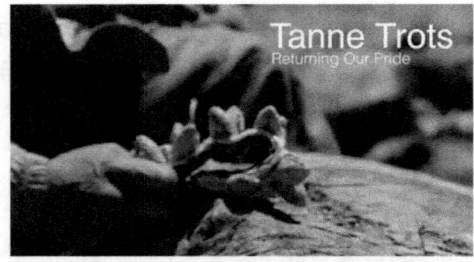

Southern African Creation Story of the San Bushman God !Kagan.
After searching for and finding First Nation stories to tell my children, I found a few that I would tell them and then decided to create illustrated versions of these Bushman stories that did not exist in illustrated form nor Afrikaaps before. It was only obvious that once I illustrated them, that I would create an animation of the same story. These creations have helped others to do the same and now we have numerous people doing so in Cape Town and South Africa.

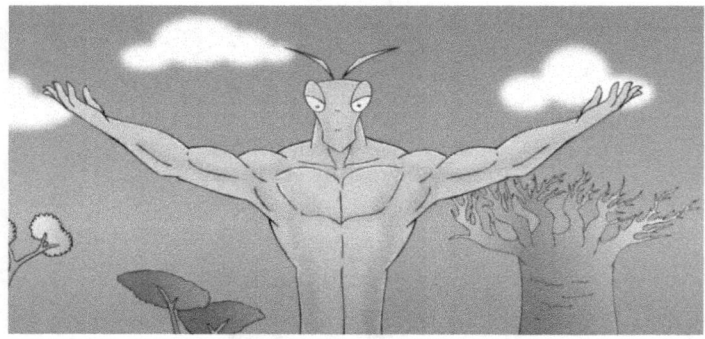

The Khoi Victory in Cape Town in 1510 (Animating OURstory)
The hidden victory of The Khoi defeating the Protuguese has always intriqued me and I wanted to show young people this story in Kaaps, in order to ensure that they would remember it and pass it on from one generation to the next. I decided to ask a young animator friend of mine to listen to a recording of the sotry that I told and to create an animation of it. It has been a huge success and copied and shared nationally on various social media platforms.

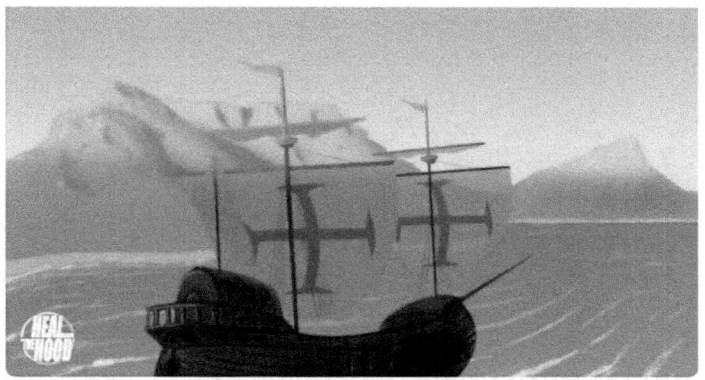

The Khoi Victory over the Portuguese, 1st March 1510 at Salt River Beach Cape Town in Kaaps ...

Break Boys

This documentary by Tamsen De Beer was created at our events and around the crews, Handbrake Turn and Ubuntu. It unfortunately focussed on beef/ disputes and so-called ghetto stereotypes, disregarding the bigger mission of Heal the Hood Project annually raising funds to send our countries best dancers to represent South Africa at Battle Of The Year in Germany. It was one of those times that we allowed people in to tell a story about our community and instead of hearing our hearts to build with us, they focussed on the divide. I only saw it that once and walked out in dissapointment after the screening.

PLAYS

Afrikaaps,
Is a Hip Hop theatre production about the black history of the creole language that was created in Cape Town and co-opted by the Afrikaaners as their own. The play takes people on a musical journey of discovery exposing the deep black origins of the language and its mixed heritage that birthed it. Dylan Valley followed the cast during the creation of the play and once we presented it to communities in Cape Town, Oudtshoorn and Holland. It captures the profound lessons learned by the cast and those who attended the play.

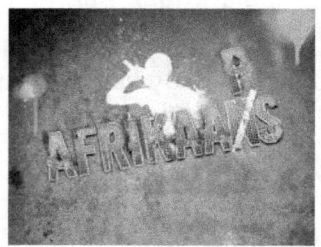

Ons Bou,
Natural Justice approached Janine, Charl and Emile to create a production about land reclamation and First Nation heritage. Emile insisted on bringing the members of *Mixed Mense* along on this journey and they not only learned about the communities struggles to reclaim land, but also the results of so many years of struggle on their minds and the lives of their children. We were coached in the Boale tradition of *Theater of The Oppressed*. It was an amazing experience that would assist the

THE CREATORS FLEX, EMILE YX?

members of Afrikaaps and Mixed Mense to use this technique for other important projects that we wished to address with our communities.

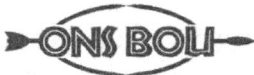

Mixing It Up,

the British Council approached me to create a Hip Hop theater play, after their UK based artist was unable to do so. I suggested that we would try to blend traditional African dance styles with Hip Hop dance styles, while recreating beats and adding the African flavour to them.

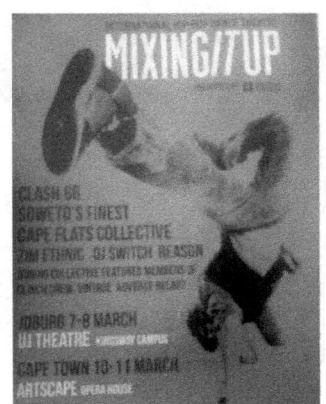

EMILE JANSEN

Stompie

This play is the result of an intensive three-week collaboration between Emile Jansen (from The Heal The Hood Project) and Kent Ekberg (representing Teater Reflex). These experienced pedagogues have a longstanding history of working within marginalized urban areas in their respective cities of Cape Town and Stockholm, utilizing dance, hip-hop, rap, and popular community theatre as powerful mediums for engagement.

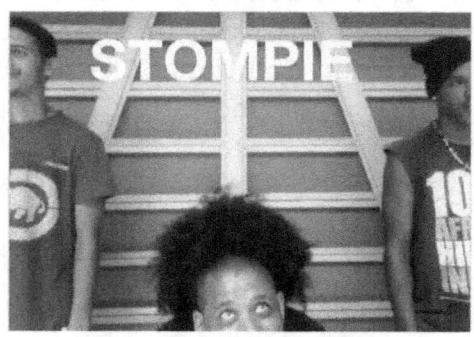

Their collaborative efforts centered around working closely with Leeroy Philips, Stefan Benting, and Andre Bozack from the Mixed Mense Collective, a group of dancers, artists, and B-boys hailing from Lavender Hill/Grassy Park. On February 25th, a work-in-progress presentation was showcased on the "Garage Stage" in Grassy Park, engaging both children and adults. The primary focus of STOMPIE has been to delve into the significance of storytelling and narrative crafting in present-day Cape Flats. This collaboration also contributes to an initiative led by Henrik Ernstson at the African Centre for Cities at UCT, emphasizing "Democratic Practices of Unequal Geographies." This broader initiative aims to expand spaces and practices dedicated to contemplating democracy and politics in Cape Town, South Africa, as well as in global South cities. Review

Die Riel van Hip Hop.

The brainchild of Shihaam Domingo and collaborative production by the artists who created the content from interesting conversations and the lessons from interactions. It was truly an amazing cast.

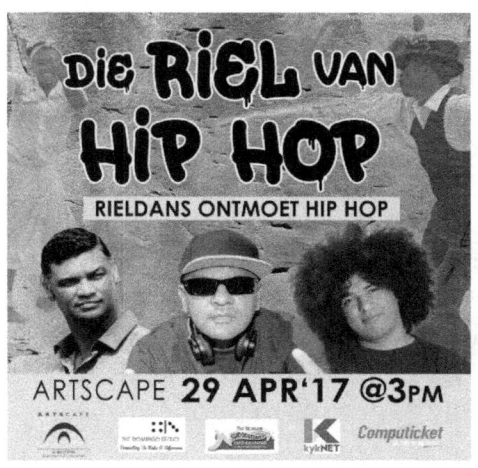

DJ Ready D, Frazer Georgio Barry , Deniel T. Barry, Camillo Robert Lombard, TopDog SA4, Die Betjies van Betjiesfontein, Emile YX?, Zenobia Klopper, Vito Heyn, Jerome Rex Des-Lee McKenzie, Hakkiesdraad Hartman, Dr. Willa Boezak, Karen Meiring, Lauren Snyders Hannie , Elton Landrew, Amy Hendrickse, Last Born Pictures, Mak1one

TEACHING & SPEAKING

Many people are unaware that I am a qualified school teacher and taught at Battswood Primary in Gosport Road, Wynberg from 1989 -1992. Although teaching prepared me to speak in front of my class, it was Hip Hop Culture that gave me the preparation to speak in front of huge groups in public spaces.

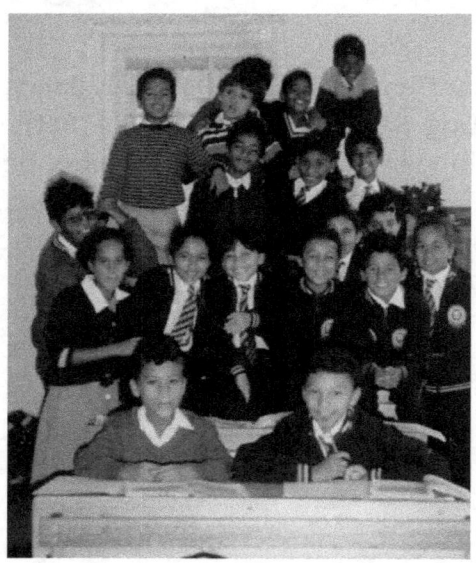

I have been invited to teach & speak at various universities and schools over the many years of my career. It was a tour of Sweden that allowed me to see the power of knowing ones own heritage and culture in order to present talks and respond to questions at various schools and universities globally.

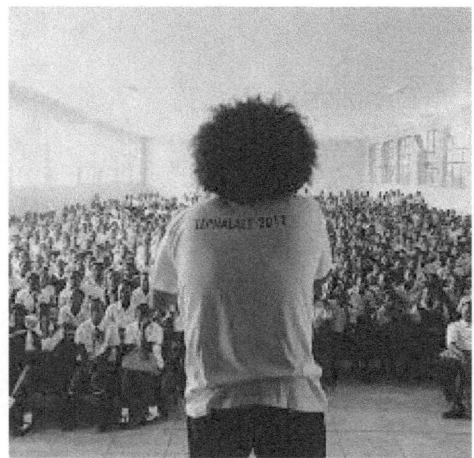

School Tour in Lephalale in Northern South Africa

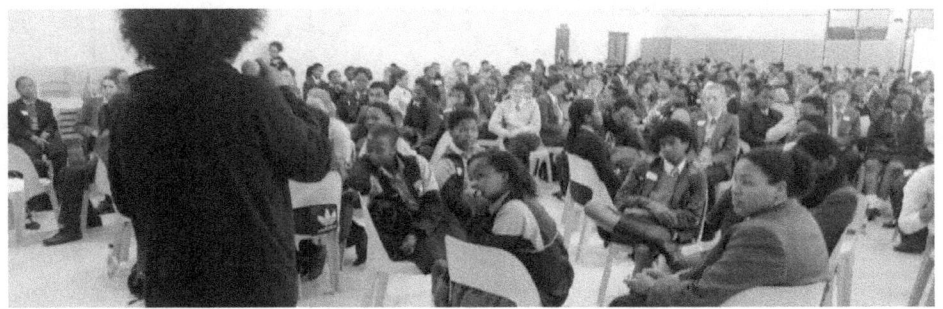

Conversations about African Pride and Selfworth

I have been invited to speak at the University of California, **Stanford 5th Element Conference,**

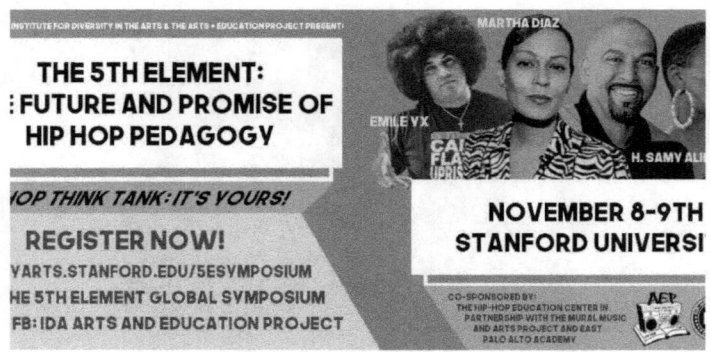

Harvard, **University of San Francisco,**

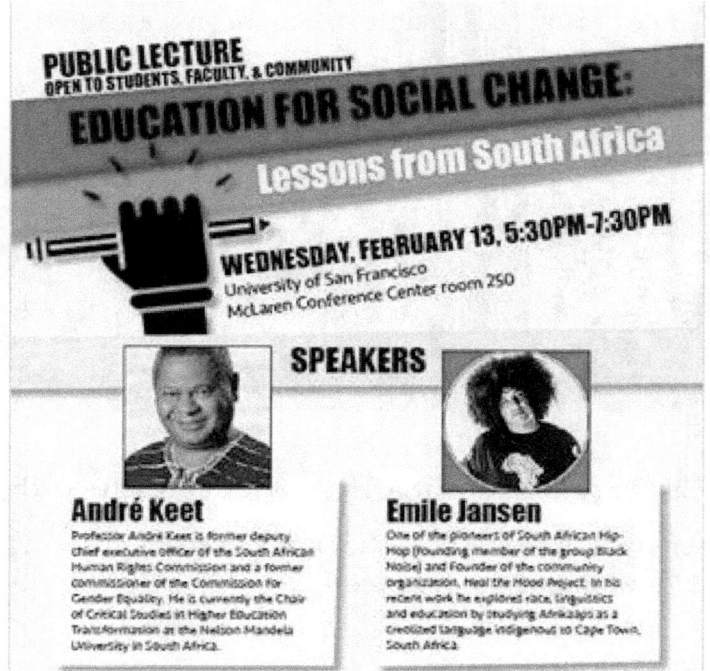

Duke, NYC, **Sacramento State University** Teachers College,

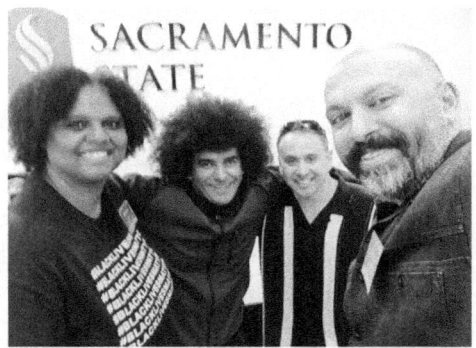

Trinity University International Hip Hop Festival,

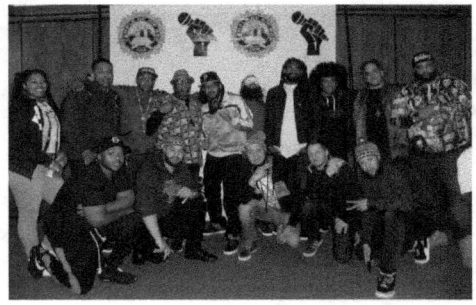

Gothenberg University, University of Cape Town, **University of the Western Cape**

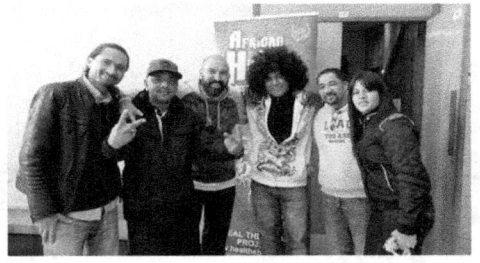

University of Washington State

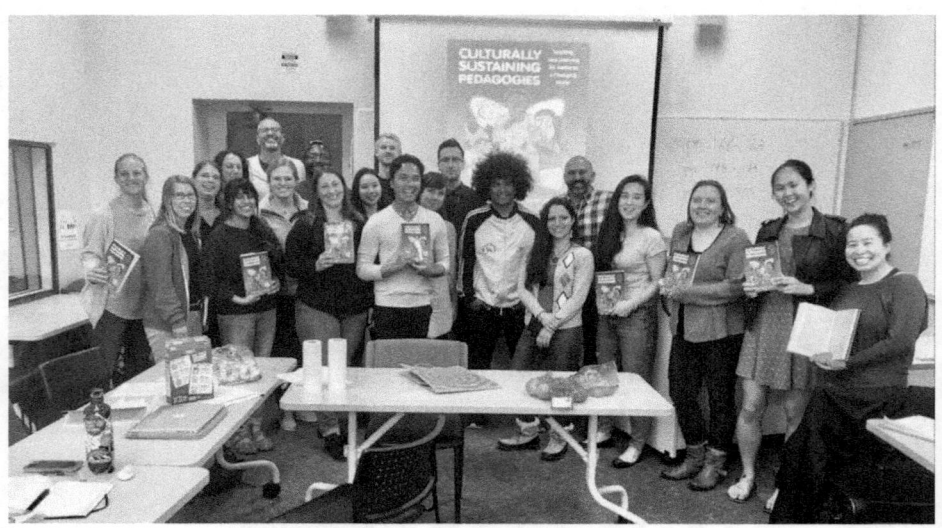

Howard University Celebrating Hip Hop's 50th

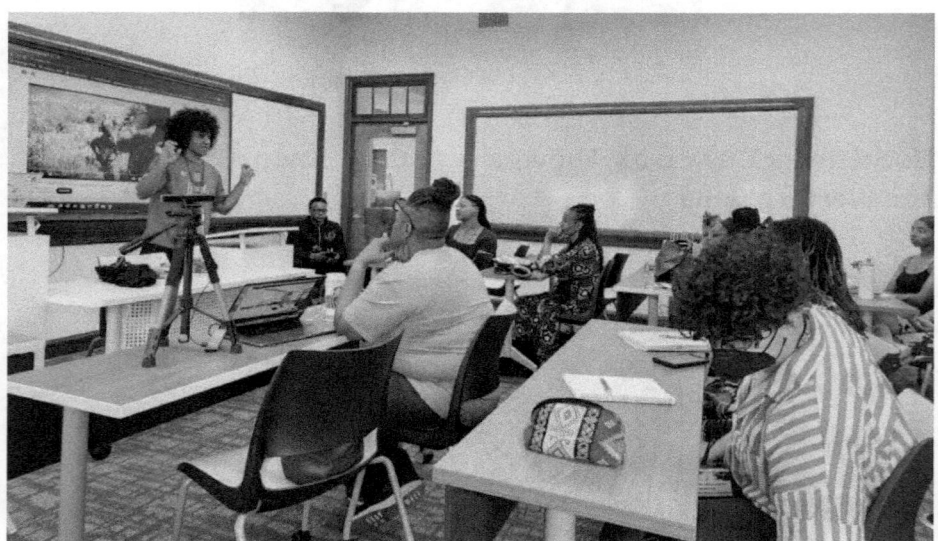

I was invited to be the artist-in-residence at **Stanford** and **University of California, Los Angeles**.

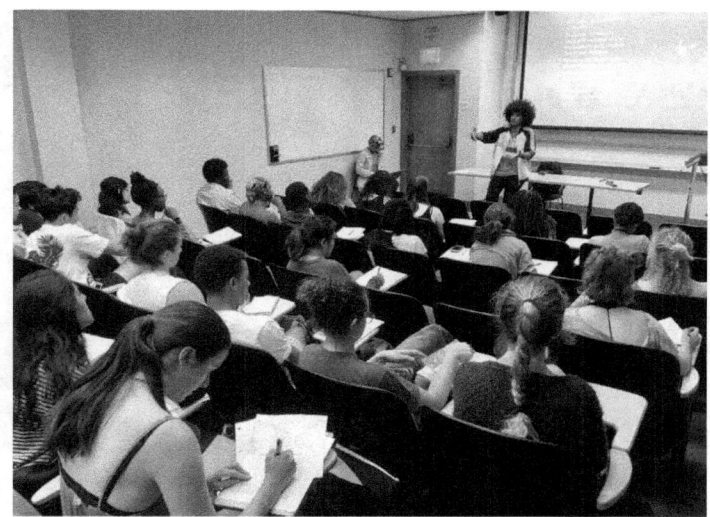

I was also invited to the African Hip Hop Summit that was hosted by **Harvard University**

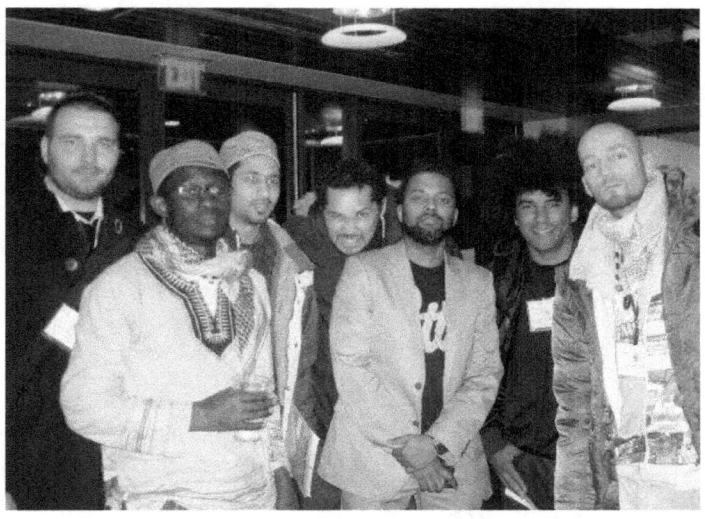

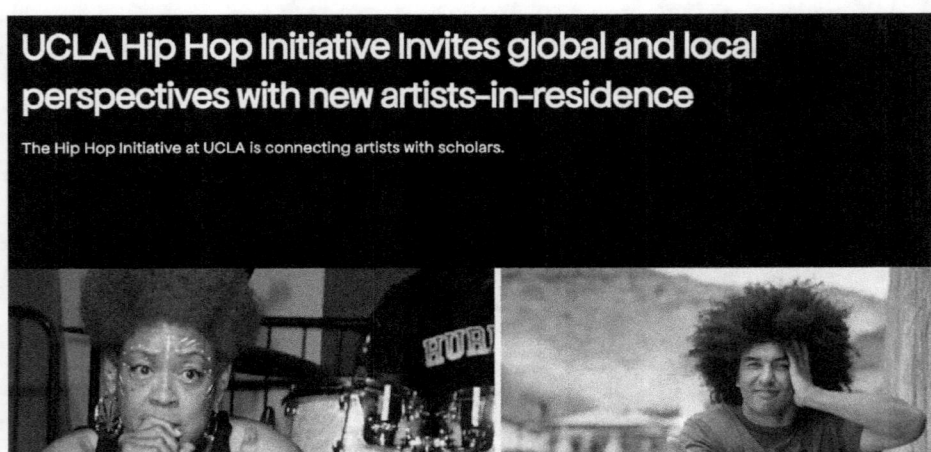

Medusa Gangsta Goddess and Emile YX? at **UCLA**

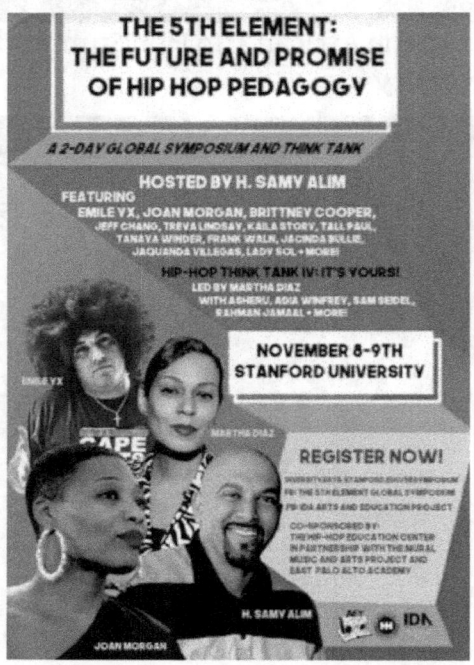

Presenting at 5th Element event at **Stanford University**

AWARDS

In May of 2024 I was awarded with the **National Order of Ikhamanga** in Silver by President of South Africa, Cyril Ramaphosa

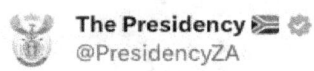

The Presidency
@PresidencyZA

President @CyrilRamaphosa, Grand Patron of the #NationalOrders bestows the Order of Ikhamanga in Silver to Mr. Emile Lester Jansen.

The Order of Ikhamanga is awarded to South African citizens who have excelled in the fields of arts, culture, literature, music, journalism, or sport.

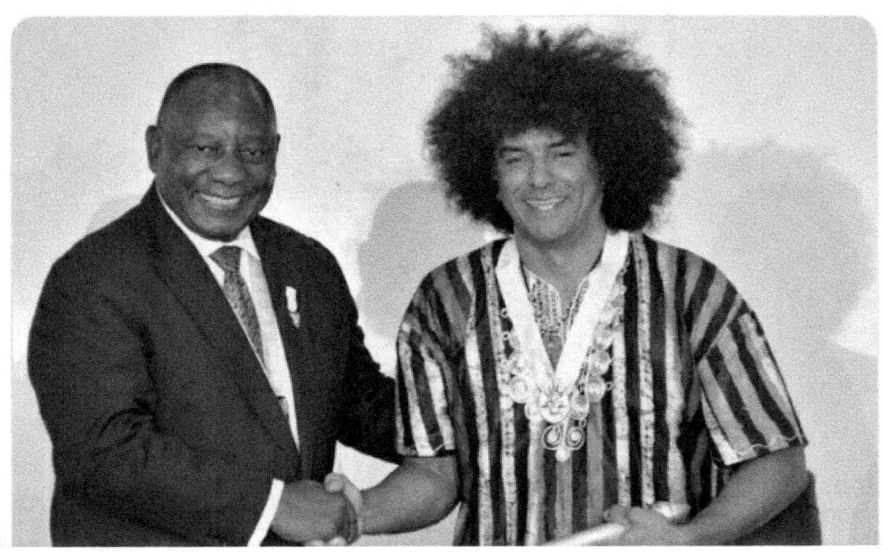

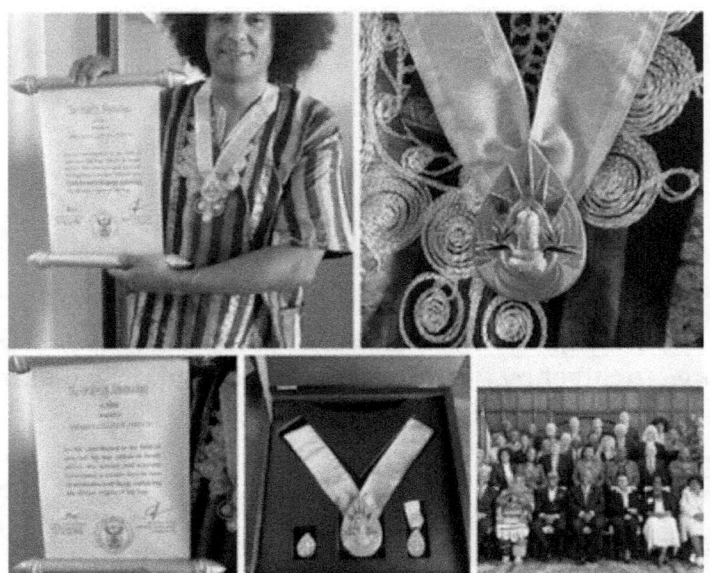

South African Hip Hop Museums Hall Of Fame.

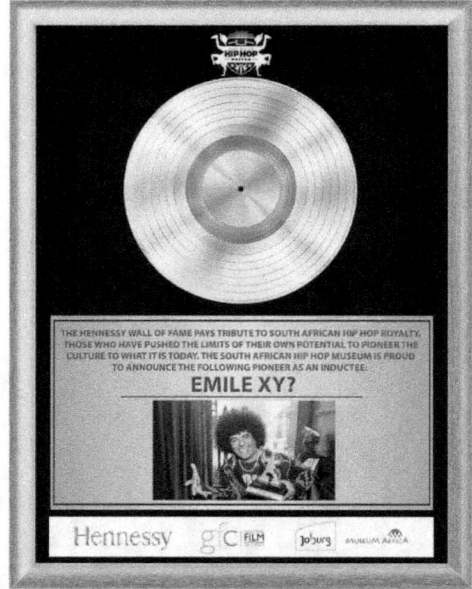

I also received an ***Honorary Award*** &

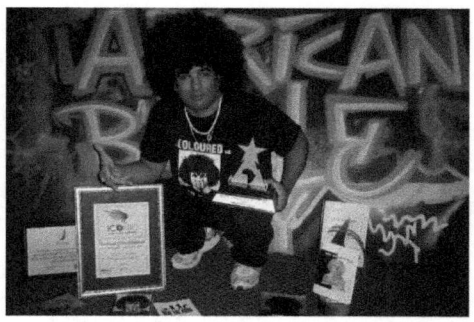

Ubuntu Activism Award from the *South African Hip Hop Awards*.

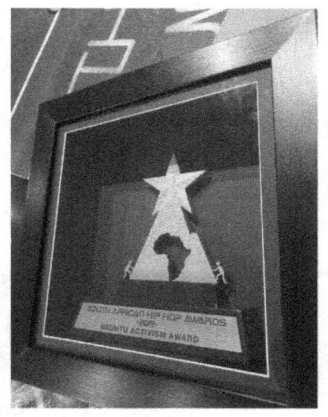

My first major award was in 1988 when I was part of the Black Noise crew that made it to the *Regional finals of the Shell Road To Fame*. Other awards were *The Mayor's Award* for Black Noise song about *Greening The City*. In 1993 Black Noise song *A Day After* reached Number 1 on Metro FM.

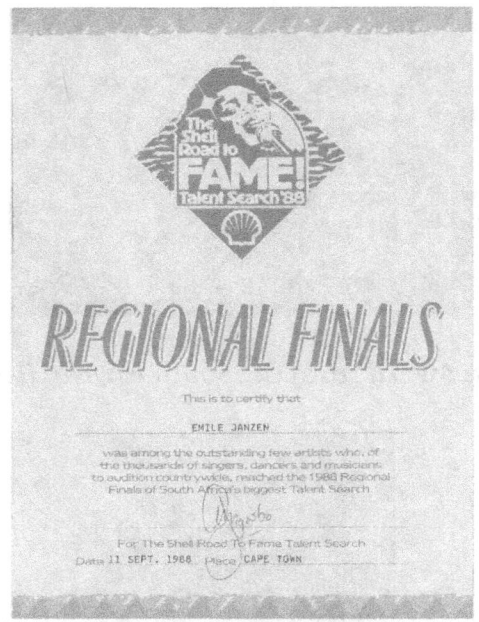

Black Noise Award at **Shell Road To Fame** 1988

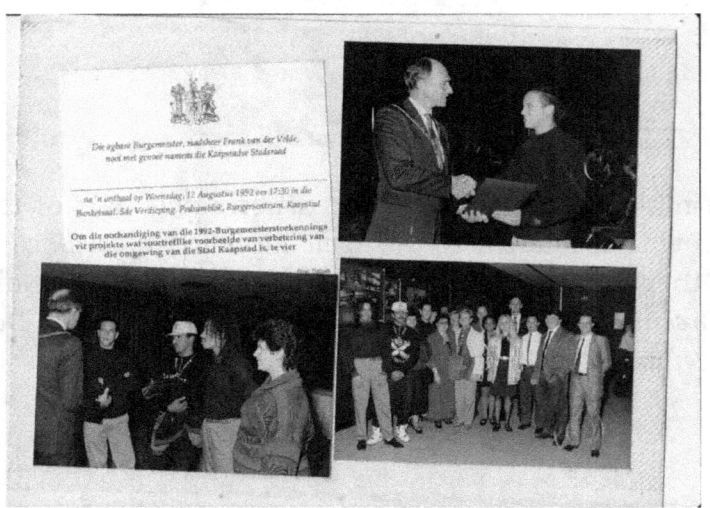

Black Noise Mayors Award for Arbor Day Song

He also won a *Lifetime Achievement Award from Iconic Urban Dance Awards* for his solo contributions to Hip Hop Dance & Culture, as well as **Black Noise winning a Lifetime Achievement Award.**

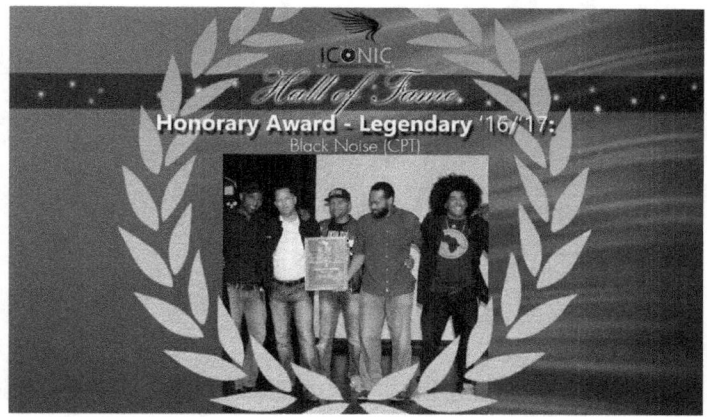

He also won the **Regional** & **National** *LeadSA Award, ETV South African Heroes Award, Mandela Monday Award,*

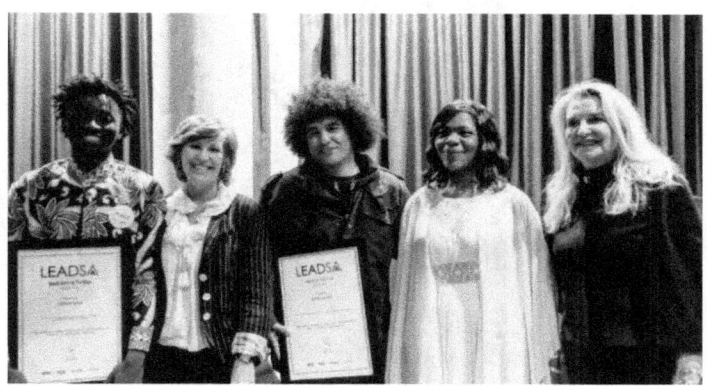

Arts & Culture Award for contributions to Literature, Blunt Magazine Award for *Activist Of the Year, Words, Beats & Life Awarded Heal the Hood Project with Best Hip Hop Organization 2009, while I was nominated for Pioneer Of The Year 2013.*

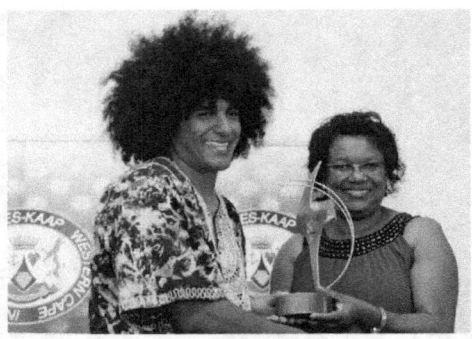

I was honoured as the face of *Moshito Music* **Conference** & awarded. I made *The Mail & Guardian list of top 300* young people to take to lunch in 2009.

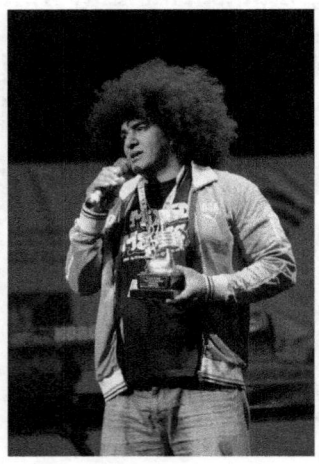

In 2022 I won the ***Distinguished Public Award from the American Association for Applied Linguistics,*** the *Living Legend Award* **from the Global dance Supreme Organization,** was selected as an *Atlantic Fellow for Racial Equity* and as **2023 UCLA Hip Hop Initiative Artist-in-Residence.**

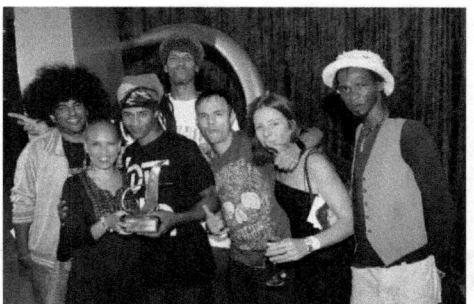

Afrikaaps Award Winning Play

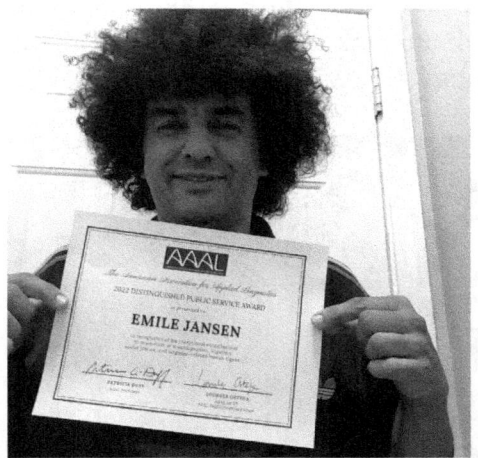

Distinguished Public Award from the American Association for Applied Linguistics

SHARING STAGES
MEETING FAMOUS ARTISTS & PEOPLE

Emile has been able to share stages with President Nelson Mandela, Dr Alan Boesak, Afrika Bambaata, **Kool DJ Herc**, Cold Crush Crew, Prince Ken Swift ...

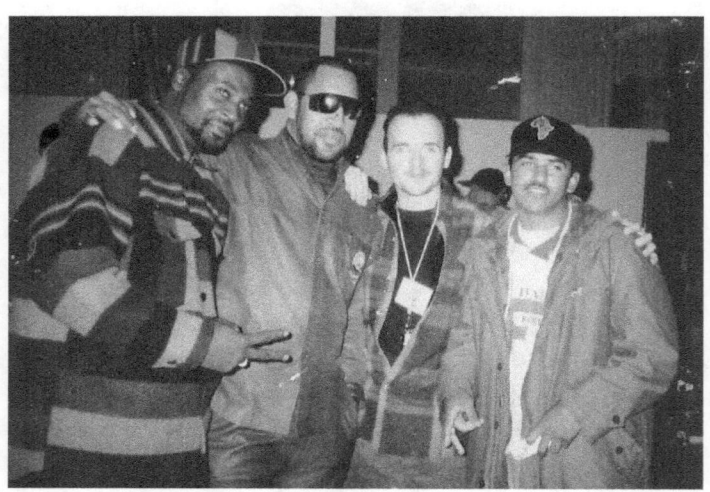

President Jacob Zuma, The Queen Of Sweden, Robbie Jansen, Tony Schilder, Hilton Schilder, Prophets of Da City, Manu Dibungo, Salif Keita, Baba Maal, Lemmy Special, Brenda Fassie, Shabba Ranks, Dr Alban, Duran Duran, 2Unlimited, Snoop Doggy Dog, Pharrell, Joe, Shaggy, Mario, **Arrested Development**,

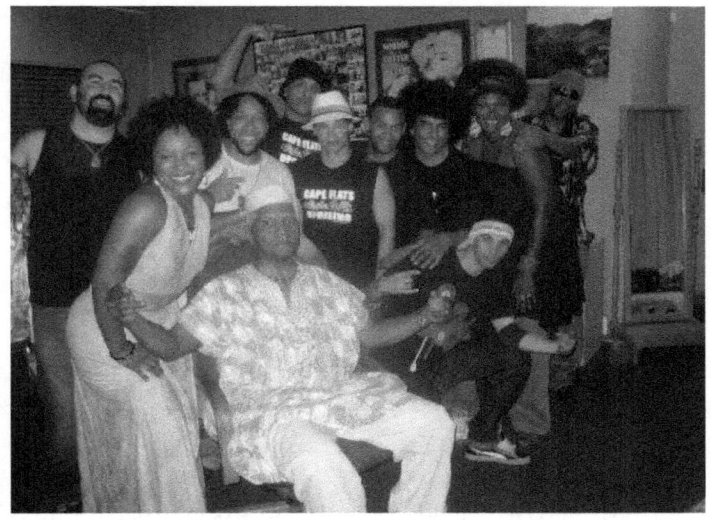

Die Antwoord, Kurt Darren, Jack Parow, Steve Hoffmeyer, Black Thought, Talib Kweli, Dead Prez,

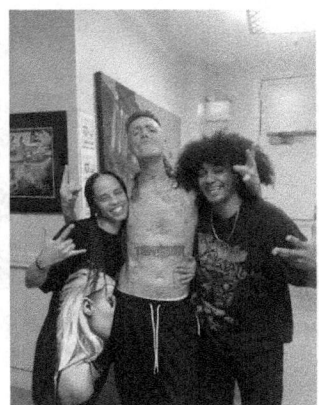

Lukmaan & Emo Adams, Shane Cooper, Kyle Shepherd, Jitsvinger, Blaq Pearl, Bliksemstraal, Moenier Monox Adams, Vicky Sampson, Jennifer Jones, Zane Adams, K'naan, **YoungstaCPT**,

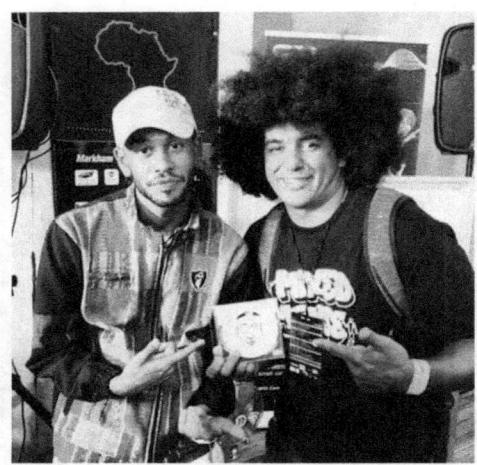

Dr Victor, Freshly Ground, The Rasta Rebels, Sons of Selassie, Marc Alex, Walk This Way, Smoking Brass, The Usual, Syndicate Sisters, AK 47, Sisters In Command, Jam B, **Canibus**,

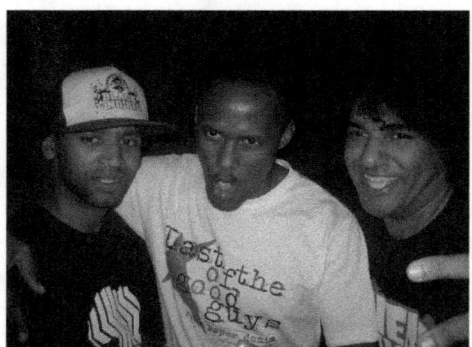

Chuck D of Public Enemy

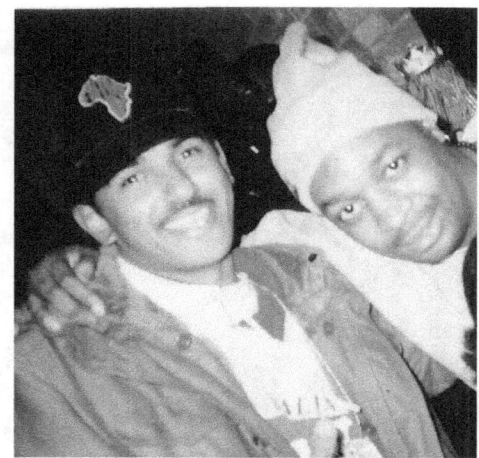

Brother Ali

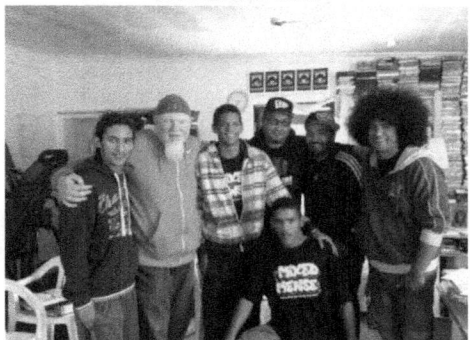

Stogie T,

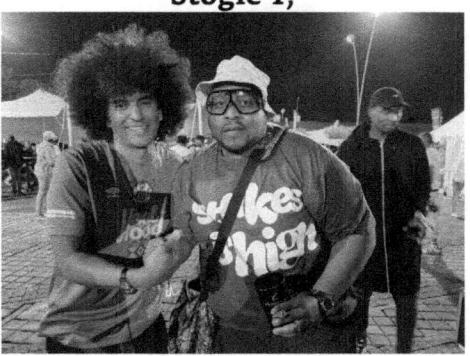

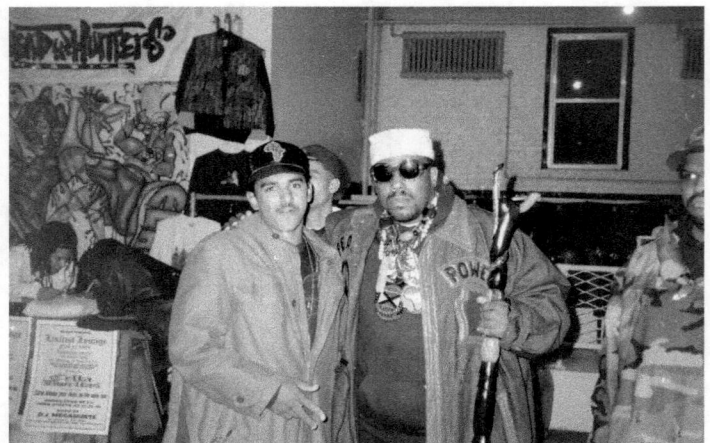
Afrika Bambaataa

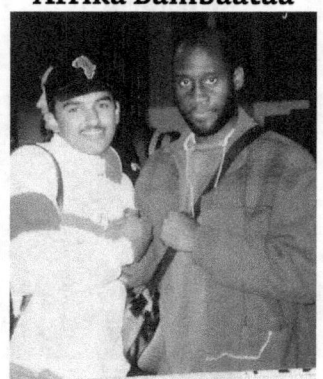
Pasdanous from De La Soul

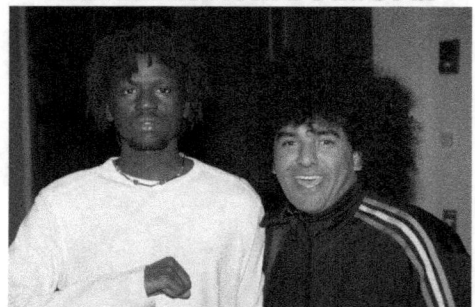
Emmanuel Jel

SPORTS ACHIEVEMENT

I believe that all my experiences shape me, so I added these sports ones. I won my *Western Province Board Baseball Squad colours*, as well as my *Western Province Board Soccer Colours* 1982. I was the captain **Devonshire Rovers Under 15 Soccer tournament winners held at Cape District in *1983*.**

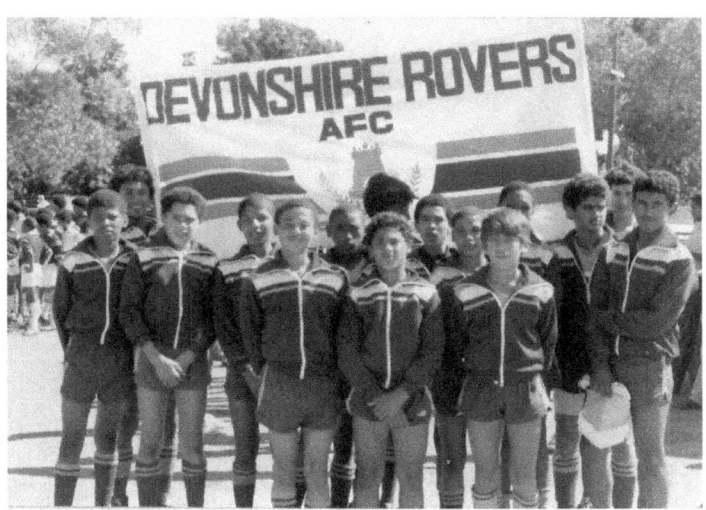

We won th**e** *first breakdancing competition* **held at Club Route 66,** Mitchells Plain.

EMILE JANSEN

At 15 years old his street Roller-Hockey Team, **Road Warriors, drew 1-1 with the all white Western Province Men's Roller-Hockey team at the M.S.A. Roller-skating competition** at Good Hope Centre on the 5th March 1983. The next year he *set the new roller-rink high jump record for Under 16* at "Fun City".

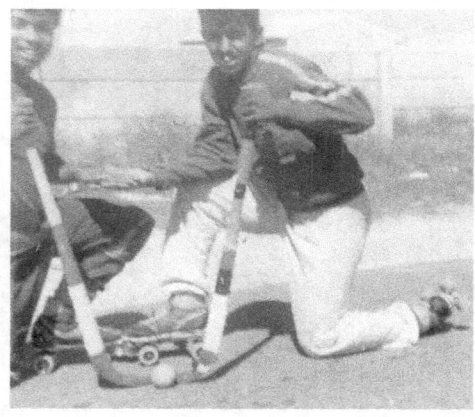

In 1986 I won the *South African Tertiary Institution Sports Associations (S.A.T.I.S.A.) colours for Javelin.* **In 1987 he won first place for Javelin** in the ***Western Province Training Colleges Sports Union,*** while setting new record in Javelin, Shot Put & Discus for Wesley College of Education.

WESTERN PROVINCE TRAINING COLLEGES SPORTS UNION

Diploma

This is to certify that

E. JANSEN (WESLEY)

gained **First** position

in the MEN U19 JAVELIN

held at VYGIESKRAAL

on 12 MARCH 1987

Time/Distance/Height 48,58 m Date 12 MARCH 1987

President Secretary

In 1988 he was a member of the *winning tertiary institution team at the SATISA soccer tournament* held in Port Elizabeth.

EMILE JANSEN

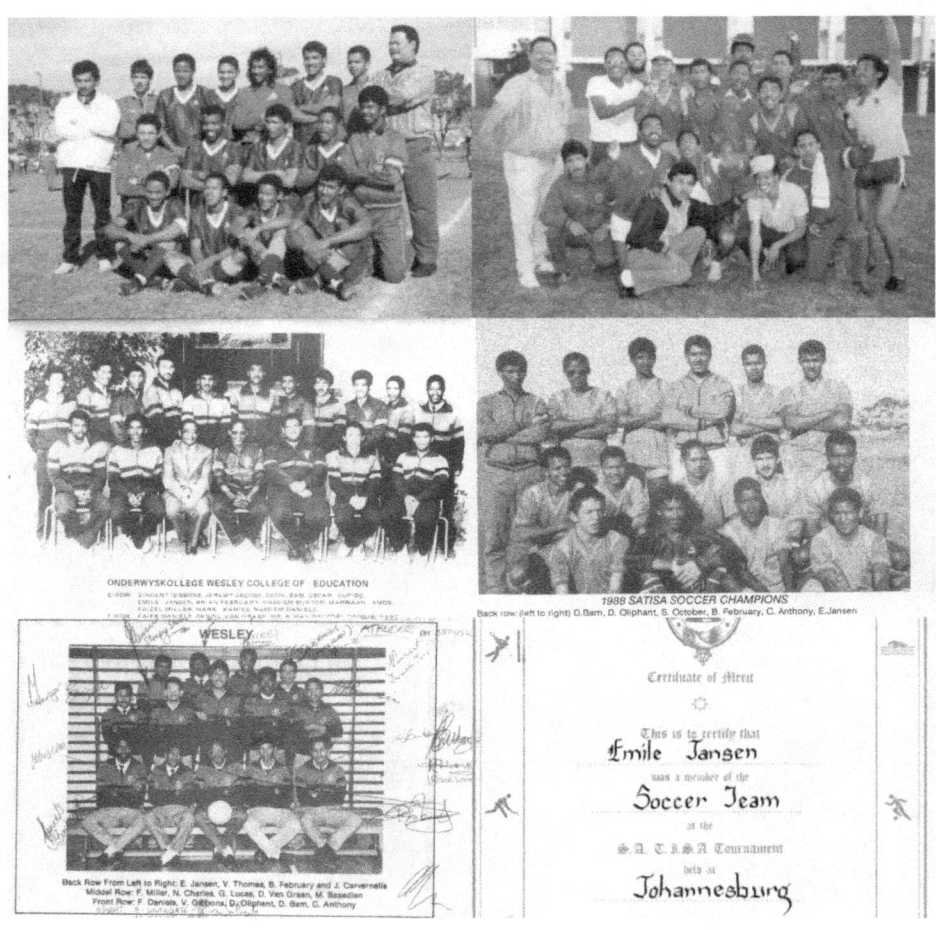

In *1998 I **brought ABADA Capoeira to Cape Town.***

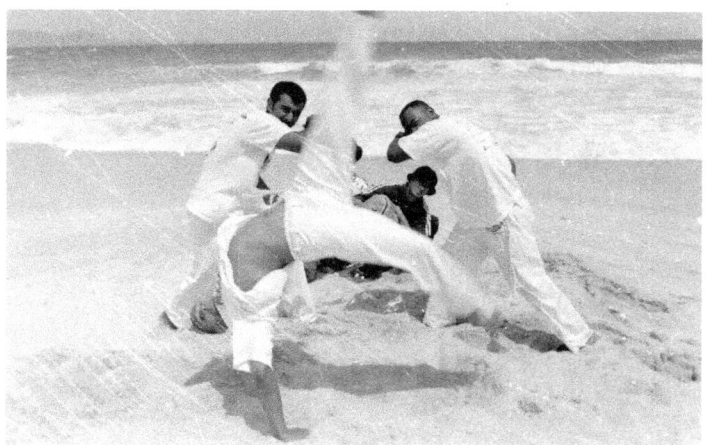

Black Noise doing **Capoeira** at Mnandi Beach

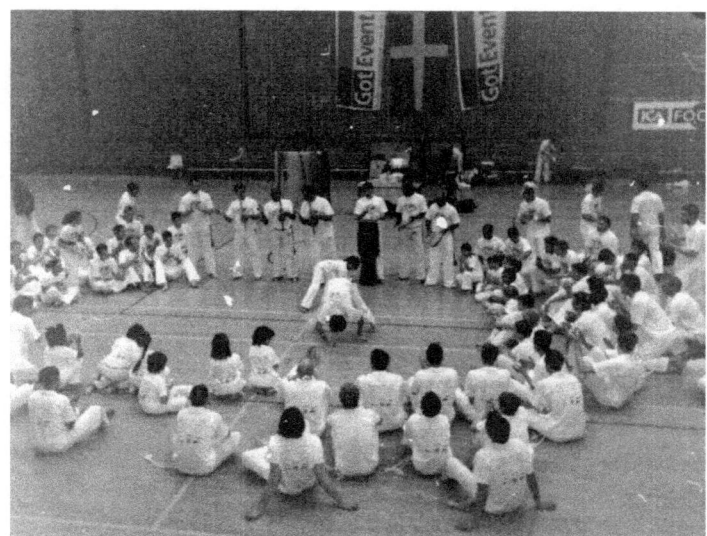

Abada Capoeira Batizado in Sweden

AFTERWORD

In sharing these actions I am hoping to inspire others to take action on their words and see Hip Hop Culture as an activator of thoughts and demanding action on their words they speak. I am also fully aware of the power of reminding oneself to continue to create and celebrate what was already achieved.

I often feel that it is in the celebration and remembering that space can be made for new creations and new ideas. We learn from our past and from the realities that young people are faced with these days. The current generation is powerful beyond measure and often when we engage and learn from them by showing that we are open to learning in these new ways, we will find that we are renewed and rebirthed in a new time. I have learned so much from the members of Mixed Mense and from the facilitators and students in Heal The Hood Programme at our various schools.

As I complete this afterward, I am about to return to South Africa to tour schools and host the ***Inaugural Hip Hop As Healing Festival in South Africa***, while inviting Hip Hop Educators from the USA to share their lessons with us. Change is never easy, but it is necessary.

I have pivoted many times. When I was afraid to enter the circle, I did so with my crew at first and then when my confidence grew, it became easier. When our lead rapper, *Caramel,* decided to leave Black Noise, I had to step up to the plate to write lyrics, I did so and added the flavour of the original B-boys to the show. When Michael of Black Noise said that we had to decide to be in the same boat with everyone else, without the life-jacket of job security, it was a moment to pivot from disbelief in self and belief in collective ability. When I looked my school principal in the eyes and told him that I quit and am going to follow my passion, it took so much bravery and desire to pivot from the overwhelming norm I was used to. When we toured the country with friends cars and set up our own shows nationally without management nor record deal. When we were but two B-boys who never made calls to clubs for shows before and rehearsed to each other, before making the calls. When the club owners directed us to our first management called Making Music Productions. When the first members of Black Noise decided to return to their jobs and leave Black Noise, we pivoted to create something new. When we went from school to school and library to library to teach the elements of Hip Hop Culture. When I created the first Hip Hop event and pivoted from waiting for others to do so for us, we would pivot and create "Do For Self".

When we raised the money to represent South Africa at the World Breaking Championships in Germany and won 3rd in the World, we pivoted from the safety of waiting to creating a solution. We would pivot from being concerned about ourselves and open the opportunities to others to experience the same thing and instead of having them be stuck with the buren of raising the funds for their flights. we raised the money or helped them to do so to the extent of raising funds for more than 250 artists.

We would again pivot by touring ourselves internationally and even be the first to get a cassette release deal and later a record deal internationally, in the USA and Sweden. Life is about taking the chances and putting yourself into situations that seems unfamiliar, but with time, just like with entering the circle and rehearsing enough in order to not be shy, I would take on the role as manager of Black Noise and then as the creator of Heal The Hood Project and stand in front of students at Harvard, Stanford and many other universities to lecture about my lessons that I have learned. When a news reporter insulted Breaking on the South African news, I promised that I would one day create a means for people to get an alternative version of what Hip Hop Culture is all about. This publication would become Da Juice, South Africa's first Hip Hop Culture magazine.

I would learn from the experience of signing a record deal that its over-rated and that I could eventually release 13 albums for Black Noise and 14 for my solo recordings. It was in listening to the audience after a show in Sweden about their difficulty in hearing all the words I was saying and how they would love to buy a copy of the lyrics, that I created my first book. I would later write articles and chapters for numerous publications, including academic papers. I remember being called to participate in a play about the black history of Afrikaans and I immediately thought two things: (1) I am not an actor and (2) I do not speak the standard version of Afrikaans that is considered respectable for the theater.

If I had walked away and allowed those two initial thoughts to dominate in my mind, I would not have learned a whole new lesson about Afrikaans and the related Bushman histories that I did by participating in the process. If I did not sing to my children and travel away from them between countries, I would never have recorded myself singing lullabies nor write bedtime stories for my children. If I did not sing them to sleep I would not have been confronted with the racist legacy of the songs we choose to sing to our babies. I pivoted away from what was comfortable and my norm to experience new things. It is not in the accomplishment of something new that we grow, but in the numerous times that we try to get it right. Those times when I tried spinning on my head after laerning to stand on my head and thinking that I would never get it right, until I kept trying and trying, over and over, again and again. Some may call it failing, I like the word **trying,** because it is human nature. It is why our children ask *why* repeatedly. It is because we are fundamentally hard-wired to learn and then it is taught out of us. When we pivot, we are not leaving something, but seeking new ways to reach the calling we were sent to explore.

It is like a game of chess, where we need to approach the probem from various angles and directions requiring us to think a few moves ahead for ourselves as well as our opponents.

In closing, I would like to remind us that we are because of others. In the same way that I listened to those around me to inspire my creations and thus fill the need, *I did not create anything without the influence of Ancestry and Community.* It is with this knowledge that I embark on a new journey of sharing and learning that is eternal. It is my dream that I will create as many things and add another book of the same length to this collection of creations.

I LOVE YOU ALL, e
5th August 2024

BOOKS BY THIS AUTHOR

My Hip Hop Is African & Proud

"My Hip Hop is African and Proud" offers an insightful overview of the African roots and global impact of hip hop culture, particularly within the context of South Africa. In this 2nd Edition of the book Emile shares a few updates and expands on a view ideas to share a more current perspectives. Here are some of the central topics addressed in the journey of Hip Hop Cultural Education and the impact of Knowledge of Self or Black / African Consciousness on the ideas and then actions of the author. Here are some of the central themes of the book:-

Exploration of African Roots: Emile YX? delves into the African origins of hip hop culture, tracing its roots back to various African traditions and musical styles. He explores how African rhythms, storytelling, and cultural practices have influenced the development of hip hop music and dance.

Global Influence: The book also examines the global impact of hip hop culture and its ability to transcend geographical boundaries. Emile YX? highlights how hip hop has become a universal language, connecting people from diverse backgrounds and cultures around the world.

Social Commentary: Through his writing, Emile YX? provides social commentary on issues such as identity, race, and inequality. He uses hip hop as a platform to address societal challenges and advocate for positive change within his community.

Personal Reflections: In addition to discussing the broader cultural significance of hip hop, Emile YX? shares personal anecdotes and reflections on his own experiences as a hip hop artist and activist in South Africa. He offers insights into the challenges and triumphs he has encountered along his journey.

Empowerment and Education: One of the central themes of the book is the power of hip hop as a tool for empowerment and education. Emile YX? emphasizes the importance of using hip hop culture as a means to uplift marginalized communities and provide opportunities for self-expression and creativity.

Overall, "My Hip Hop is African and Proud" serves as both a celebration of hip hop's African heritage and a call to action for positive social change. It offers a unique perspective on the cultural significance of hip hop and its ability to inspire and unite people across continents. Emile insists that Hip Hop Culture is. VERB, an ACTION WORD that demands its practitioners to make real their thoughts, words and movements.

Conscious Rhymes For Unconscious Times

"Conscious Rhymes For Unconscious Times" by Emile Jansen is a thought-provoking collection of poetry that delves into the complexities of contemporary society, exploring themes of identity, social justice, and personal transformation. Through powerful verse and vivid imagery, Jansen invites readers to confront the pressing issues of our time with honesty and introspection.

Drawing from his own experiences as a South African artist and activist, Jansen's poetry resonates with authenticity and passion. He skillfully navigates topics such as inequality, racism, and cultural heritage, challenging readers to examine their own beliefs and biases while inspiring them to work towards a more just and equitable world.

At its core, "Conscious Rhymes For Unconscious Times" is a call to action, urging readers to awaken their consciousness and engage with the world around them in meaningful ways. Whether reflecting on the struggles of marginalized communities or celebrating the resilience of the human spirit, Jansen's poetry offers a powerful reminder of the transformative power of art and the enduring quest for social change.

A Colouredful Life: The Naughty Kid Years

"A Colouredful Life: Part 1 - The Naughty Kid Years (Die Stoutgat Jare)" offers a unique perspective on the experience of being labeled 'Coloured' during the Apartheid era in South Africa. In this collection of short stories, we delve into the early life of Emile Jansen, set against the backdrop of Grassy Park, Cape Town.

Emile's narrative begins with a lighthearted look at his mischievous antics as a naughty kid during challenging times. These stories are predominantly told in English but are infused with the colorful and expressive language of Kaaps, or Afrikaaps, a Creole tongue born from the multicultural roots of Cape Town.

Within these pages, Emile shares 24 carefully selected stories that encompass the very fabric of his upbringing. We journey from his birth to his parents, family, and the tight-knit community that shaped his formative years.

The stories touch on key aspects of Emile's early life, from the neighborhood he was born into (Waar ko' djy vandaan) to the profound importance of greetings in his community (groet is 'n moet). The tales explore themes of resourcefulness, sharing, and even the audacious act of pilfering food (kos gangsters).

Emile's childhood adventures take us on a whimsical ride, from getting his uncle's chickens inebriated (Gesuipte Honders) to becoming a 'dart-wielding ninja' and navigating the dynamics of weekends on the vibrant Cape Flats.

Prepare to be both entertained and enlightened as Emile brings to life the charm, humor, and resilience that defined his early years. "A Colouredful Life: Part 1 - The Naughty Kid Years" is a heartwarming and hilarious journey into a world that may be foreign to some but is filled with universal themes of laughter, growth, and the shared experiences of childhood.

Reconnect The String

"Reconnect The String" by Emile YX? is a groundbreaking exploration that unveils the profound ancestral connections between Hip-Hop culture and its First Nation / African origins. Through a tapestry of shared expressions and narratives, this transformative book illuminates the hidden threads that bind us, ultimately leading to a global community united by talent, skills, and the reclamation of our shared humanity and kinship. The cyclic chants and clapping of the ancient ones around the fire is compared to the selected break beats that were looped to drive the dancers into trance. Those very breaks that birthed the breakdancer or b-boy can be compared to the trance dancer driven into that state for healing. The story tellers are compared to the rappers or MC's. The rock art of old to the aerosol art or wrongly named graffiti of today and the circle is the portal where time stands still and we bring down the sky to reconnect the string to who we truly are.

Emile YX?, an eminent pioneer of South African Hip-Hop hailing from Cape Town, South Africa, delves deep into the very essence of Hip-Hop Culture in "Reconnect The String." Drawing inspiration from the profound wisdom of Bushman thought, the book emphasizes how our disconnection from our past, present, and future has left us estranged from ourselves, our spirits, and the natural world.

At its core, "Reconnect The String" champions the power of first-person narratives and the retelling of our own heritage. Emile YX? passionately recounts local stories, inviting readers to reclaim their own histories. The journey commences in Cape Town and extends globally, as the author encourages readers worldwide to join hands in reweaving their stories and revitalizing their cultural legacies.

More than a book, "Reconnect The String" is an odyssey of authentic connections, unveiling the authentic camaraderie and familial bonds that thrive within the Hip-Hop community, transcending industry barriers. In a world where information is often colonized, this work endeavors to restore the heart and soul of Hip-Hop. By tracing the lineage of a culture deeply rooted in Africa, the cradle of humanity, Emile YX? advocates for the rehumanization of information and the resurgence of a global heritage that speaks to us all.

Don't miss the chance to experience "Reconnect The String" and embark on a transformative journey to reclaim our heritage, rewrite our histories, and reignite the heart of Hip-Hop culture. Embrace the power of unity, self-expression, and the timeless legacy that binds us all.

www.ingramcontent.com/pod-product-compliance
Lightning Source LLC
Chambersburg PA
CBHW050327230526
45471CB00005B/2384